In the Line of Inquiry

Solving the Unsolvable

By
Jeff A. Schwarz

In the Line of Inquiry

Solving the Unsolvable

Table of Contents

Introduction

Step into the labyrinthine world of criminal investigation, a realm where stories of deception, betrayal, and justice unfold. Here, the stakes are high—often involving life and death—and the heroes and heroines wield a mix of intuition, skill, and dogged determination. This journey through the intricacies of crime-solving isn't just for the experienced detectives featured in your favorite crime dramas; it's for anyone intrigued by the human psyche, legal systems, and the relentless pursuit of truth.

The art of solving crimes has fascinated people for centuries. It intertwines numerous disciplines, each contributing a unique perspective to the ever-evolving tapestry of detecting wrongdoing. This book unravels the complexities behind this pursuit, offering insights into the methodologies and technologies that professionals use to bring criminals to justice. From forensic science breakthroughs to psychological profiling, every chapter peels back another layer of this multifaceted field.

Consider the value of forensic science, where the human body's silent testimony to violence often holds the key to solving cases. Analysis of physical evidence can shed light on events shrouded in mystery, giving voice to the victims who can no longer speak for themselves. And then there's the role of criminal psychology, which finds patterns in the chaos, allowing investigators to piece together fragments of the perpetrator's mind.

Crime scene analysis stands as a testament to the meticulous nature of investigations. The tiniest thread or misplaced object can unravel an entire mystery. Investigators walk a delicate balance between scientific rigor and artistic interpretation, needing to be creative, disciplined, and intuitive all at once. Each case becomes a unique puzzle, its pieces scattered across a timeline of human behavior.

In the realm of interrogation and interviews, psychological acumen is crucial. Beyond the memorized scripts and rehearsed answers lies the truth, hidden under layers of fear, guilt, or misinformation. Effective communication is key; the right question asked at the right moment can unravel deceptive narratives and reveal the elusive facts.

Technology has become an indispensable ally in modern investigations, revolutionizing how evidence is collected, analyzed, and presented. Surveillance tools and digital forensics have expanded the reach of investigators, breaking geographical barriers and delving into cyber realms. And yet, this expansion comes with its own set of ethical dilemmas, challenging investigators to balance innovation with privacy concerns.

Finally, this journey isn't confined to local precincts or national borders. The global landscape of crime-solving demands cooperation and coordination across jurisdictions, cultures, and legal systems. Sharing knowledge and expertise enriches the global fight against crime, uniting professionals in their relentless pursuit of justice.

This introduction serves as the gateway to a detailed exploration of crime-solving. Whether you're a seasoned enthusiast or someone newly captivated by the process, this book invites you to engage deeply with the science, art, and humanity at the heart of every investigation. As each chapter unfolds, may you find inspiration in the stories of those who seek justice and the remarkable tools at their disposal.

Chapter 1:
Introduction to Criminal
Investigation

Welcome to the intricate world of criminal investigation, where curiosity meets methodical rigor, and truth peels back the layers of deceit. At the heart of every captivating whodunit lies the diligent work of investigators piecing together puzzles of human nature and circumstance. This chapter sets the stage for our journey by exploring the core principles that drive successful crime-solving efforts, revealing the evolution of techniques from rudimentary observations to today's sophisticated methodologies. From the bustling precincts of urban centers to the quieter corners of rural towns, detectives employ a blend of intuition, science, and dogged persistence in their pursuit of justice. Each case is a crucible of human emotion, bound by the threads of logic and evidence. Here, we touch on the essentials of investigation, preparing you for a deeper dive into the specialized skills and knowledge that define modern investigations. Welcome to the frontlines, where every clue counts, and every detail could crack the case wide open.

Fundamentals of Crime-Solving

The fundamentals of crime-solving are the bedrock that supports the entire field of criminal investigation. They embody the skills, methods, and approaches polished over centuries, which investigators rely on when piecing together the complexities of a crime. Essentially, these fundamentals are a combination of art and science, a blend of intuition and empirical study.

At the heart of crime-solving lies the ability to observe. Observation is perhaps the most undervalued skill, yet it is indispensable. Detectives must train themselves to notice details that others might overlook. Think of Sherlock Holmes with his keen eye, picking up on the slightest things that eventually unravel the mystery. In the real world, this could be anything from the placement of a chair to a peculiar scent in the air. Keen observation feeds into situational awareness, allowing investigators to reconstruct events with striking accuracy.

Another cornerstone in crime-solving is logical reasoning. When an investigator embarks on unraveling a case, they start with known facts and layer them with hypotheses. Through deduction and sometimes induction, they can carve a believable narrative of the criminal activity. In many respects, solving a crime is like assembling a jigsaw puzzle. Pieces might appear incongruent at first, but with rigorous analysis and an expansive view of available data, a clearer picture emerges.

Documentation is the silent hero that bolsters every investigation. From the initial report to the final draft submitted in court, every detail must be meticulously recorded. Precise documentation can make or break a case. Investigators know that even a fleeting oversight can be seized upon by defense lawyers, leading to reasonable doubt. Therefore, they leave no stone unturned, ensuring that evidence is cataloged methodically and narratives are supported by unassailable records.

Collaboration forms the backbone of successful investigations. Crime-solving is rarely a solitary pursuit. Police departments, forensic experts, psychologists, and legal teams constantly exchange information and insights to keep the flame of justice burning bright.

An overlooked entity in this network is often the public itself. Communities can serve as additional eyes and ears, providing crucial leads that propel investigations forward.

Then, there's the human factor. The field of criminal investigation is one where empathy and psychological insight are invaluable. Understanding the mind of the victim, as well as the perpetrator, goes a long way in revealing motives and framing potential suspects. Investigators often delve into the psyche of criminals, picking apart their backgrounds, triggers, and signatures to predict future actions and identify guilt. This skill becomes even more crucial when engaging with victims or witnesses, where sensitivity and tact are required to gather truthful accounts.

The stakes in crime-solving are extraordinarily high, and there are inherent challenges. An investigation is rarely straightforward. Red herrings, false leads, and dead ends often litter the path to justice, demanding flexibility and open-mindedness from detectives. Successful investigators remain resolute, adaptable in their methods, ever ready to follow a sudden, surprising twist in the trail of evidence.

Technology has ushered in a new era of possibilities in crime-solving. The advent of DNA profiling, digital forensics, and surveillance technologies has empowered investigators with tools unimaginable just a few decades ago. These technological advancements are integrated seamlessly into modern investigative processes, complementing traditional methods rather than replacing them. However, technology's influence is vast, and understanding its multifaceted role is crucial for modern investigators, a topic explored in greater detail in later chapters.

Yet, even with all these advancements, the importance of foundational skills—empathy, observation, reasoning—remains undiminished. They provide the lens through which technology is most effectively applied, ensuring the human touch is not lost. It is this blend of timeless skills and cutting-edge tools that propels the field of criminal investigation forward.

The journey of solving a crime is often unpredictable and incredibly complex. It's a path that demands the highest degree of integrity from all involved, as oversight or misconduct can compromise not just a case, but the very trust placed in the justice system. Thus, those involved in crime-solving are ever mindful of their ethical and social responsibilities, treating each investigation with the gravity and diligence it deserves.

In understanding these fundamentals, one gains a richer appreciation of the art of crime-solving. It becomes evident that each solved case is not just a closed file but a symbol of collective triumph—a testament to the seamless integration of skill, science, and sometimes even a little luck. As we continue to unveil more techniques and explore the evolution of investigative practices, the essence of these fundamentals remains, timeless and unyielding, guiding the way toward justice.

Evolution of Investigative Techniques

Tracing the evolution of investigative techniques is akin to following the thread of human ingenuity itself. As societies have grown more complex, so too have the methods employed to unravel the mysteries of criminal activities. In the nascent days of criminal investigation, when the world was still a tapestry of local customs and oral traditions, crimes were often solved through rudimentary means. Town squares acted as courts, and justice was often meted out with a blend of folklore and fear. The evolution from such primitive methods to today's sophisticated techniques mirrors the broader trajectory of human progress.

Initially, investigative work relied heavily on the memory and intuition of local constables and sheriffs. Communities were small, and crimes often personal, which made intuition a key tool. However, as urbanization swept through Europe and America during the 19th century, a new reality dawned: crimes grew more anonymous and sophisticated. It was no longer enough to rely on memory alone. The birth of the detective as a professional role marked a pivotal shift. Figures like Eugène Vidocq in France and Sir Robert Peel in England introduced organized detective units, emphasizing the necessity of systematic approaches. They were pioneers who laid the groundwork for what would become a radical transformation in crime-solving techniques.

The late 19th century saw the inception of what we might now refer to as the scientific approach to investigation. The introduction of forensic science was revolutionary. Techniques such as fingerprinting, first used in the late 1800s, provided a new, infallible means of identifying suspects. Sir Francis Galton's work in fingerprint classification set a precedent for the use of scientific principles in law enforcement, igniting a paradigm shift that saw investigators increasingly relying on physical evidence over mere conjecture.

Yet, it wasn't just the hard sciences that influenced the evolution of investigative techniques. The development of psychological profiling emerged alongside advances in the understanding of human behavior. Inspired by the intersections of psychology and criminology, investigators began crafting profiles of unknown killers, honing in on their likely traits and backgrounds with astonishing accuracy. This interplay between psychology and investigation continues to play a crucial role, particularly in understanding and predicting the actions of serial offenders.

As we moved into the 20th century, the radio crackled to life with the intrigue of criminal dramas, capturing public imagination and pushing investigative techniques further into the realm of systemic study and organization. Agencies like the FBI and Scotland Yard emerged as bastions of investigative rigor, advancing methodologies through rigorous training programs and cross-disciplinary collaboration. The integration of technology began its upward curve here, laying the groundwork for the digital revolution that would radically reshape the landscape of investigations.

In tandem with technological advancements, legal frameworks evolved significantly during this period. The imperative to balance effective investigation with the protection of individual rights led to established protocols, standardizing the process and enhancing its legitimacy. The Miranda rights in the United States are one such example, highlighting how investigative practices were redefined to ensure fairness and constitutionality.

The second half of the 20th century brought about the computer age, fundamentally altering how crime solving occurred. The introduction of databases allowed for the rapid collation and analysis of information, enabling law enforcement agencies to connect the dots across disparate incidents with unprecedented speed and accuracy. The birth of the internet brought both challenges and opportunities; while it enabled new forms of crime, it also opened new avenues for digital investigation.

In the 21st century, the role of technology in criminal investigation can't be overstated. With the rise of tools like DNA analysis, facial recognition, and digital forensics, the canvas of criminal investigation has expanded far beyond traditional bounds. The potential to reconstruct crime scenes with 3D imaging, track the digital footprints left behind by cybercriminals, and even predict criminal activity through data analytics marks the new era of investigation where science fiction seemingly turns into reality.

But as techniques have evolved, so have the criminals. The rise of cybercrime and identity theft presents modern investigators with unique challenges that demand continual adaptation and innovation.

In tackling these problems, investigators draw on an ever-expanding toolbox, one enhanced by artificial intelligence and machine learning, which offers insights that were previously unimaginable.

This evolution has not come without ethical considerations. Surveillance technology, for example, while significantly enhancing investigative reach, raises questions about privacy and civil liberties. Balancing effective crime-solving strategies with respect for individual rights is a delicate dance that continues to demand attention and refinement.

The journey of investigative techniques is far from over. As crime continues to adapt to societal and technological changes, so too will the methods used to combat it. Future trends suggest an increasing reliance on interdisciplinary approaches, gathering insights from diverse fields such as sociology, data science, and ethics, ensuring the practice remains as much an art as it is a science. Indeed, as we look forward, the key to successful investigations may lie as much in embracing innovative technology as in harnessing the age-old art of human intuition and empathy.

Ultimately, the evolution of investigative techniques offers a fascinating window into the complexities of human society. From humble origins rooted in community wisdom to high-tech solutions leveraging global networks, the path of criminal investigation reflects a continuous dance between adaptation and innovation, forging new frontiers in the ongoing pursuit of justice.

Chapter 2:
The Role of Forensic Science

Forensic science marks the crossroads of science and law, where truth and justice converge through methodical examination of evidence. As crime scenes freeze in time, forensic experts step in to unravel the stories etched into each detail. From the microscopic imprints of fingerprints to the silent whispers captured in a strand of hair, forensic science transforms mere traces into compelling narratives. It's an intricate ballet of DNA sequencing, digital forensics, and chemical analysis, each step a leap towards clarity and conviction. The field stands as a sentinel against uncertainty in the justice system, its role invaluable and ever-evolving. By bridging the gap between the abstract world of facts and the tangible realm of law, forensic science serves not only to solve mysteries but also to prevent injustices, making it an indispensable ally in modern investigations.

Forensic Science in Modern Investigations

In the realm of modern criminal investigations, forensic science stands as the unyielding pillar upon which much of crime-solving rests. It's no longer just a mysterious science fiction concept but a well-established, critical component of justice. With every innovative stride, forensic science transforms a crime scene into a treasure trove of clues, meticulously dissecting facets of reality previously unseen. Gone are the days when crimes hinged solely on eyewitness accounts and confessions. Today, forensic scientists wield microscopes as detectives wield magnifying glasses, each particle and fiber telling a fragment of a larger story.

The breadth and scope of forensic science cover a vast array of fields, weaving a complex yet coherent tapestry of methodologies. From DNA analysis and toxicology to ballistics and digital forensics, each specialty serves as a piece of the larger puzzle. The importance of DNA profiling, for example, cannot be overstated. Since its advent, DNA testing has become one of the matchless cornerstones of forensic investigations. Its ability to connect or exonerate individuals with pinpoint accuracy has made it indispensable. Even the tiniest sample—a stray hair, a drop of sweat—can help reconstruct a narrative that was otherwise invisible to the naked eye.

However, forensic science isn't just about the physical evidence. It delves into understanding behaviors, motives, and the subtleties that often accompany human actions. Criminalistics, a branch of forensic science, involves interpreting the evidence gathered and ultimately trying to comprehend what might have transpired. This multidimensional approach ensures that each case is examined from numerous angles, providing a holistic view of the incidents on trial. Not only does it aid in criminal convictions, but it also plays an indispensable role in overturning wrongful convictions, thus safeguarding the integrity of the justice system.

Fingerprint analysis, another established technique, operates at the intersection of art and science. It's an art form in identifying patterns, and a science in preserving and interpreting those strokes of identity. In this digital age, traditional fingerprinting has evolved into digital imaging techniques which enhance prints left on a variety of surfaces—from weapons to touchscreens. These advancements mean that even the most intricately laid plans can unravel at the sight of a smudged fingerprint, forever binding the criminal to the scene of the crime.

As society plunges further into the digital era, forensic science is confronted with the burgeoning field of digital forensics. Cybercrimes have ushered in a new set of challenges and opportunities for forensic teams. Analyzing data from smartphones, computers, and online communications requires a confluence of technological prowess and investigative acumen. Whether it's tracing financial fraud through complex electronic trails or delving into the depths of cyberbullying cases, digital forensics has rapidly become a crucial area within the mosaic of scientific investigation.

A significant impact of modern forensic science lies in its capacity for collaboration across borders. Crimes aren't confined within national boundaries, and neither should be their investigations. International cooperation has become paramount in solving crimes that span multiple jurisdictions. For example, Interpol's DNA database allows countries to share and access crucial genetic data, enhancing the chances of capturing culprits who operate on a global scale. This interconnectedness not only bolsters the reach of forensic evidence but also tightens the net around those who hope to escape justice through geographical evasion.

The evolution of forensic methodologies is a testimony to human ingenuity and resilience. Each breakthrough and each refinement serves as a testament to the relentless pursuit of truth. Nevertheless, as forensic science advances, ethical considerations sprint to keep pace. Controversies about privacy, the potential for bias in testing procedures, and data handling simultaneously evolve with technological feats. It's a delicate balance, forging a path that maximizes investigative capabilities while safeguarding individual rights and freedoms.

In the courtroom, forensic evidence assumes the role of an eyewitness. It's not susceptible to the faltering memory nor swayed by emotions. It stands on facts and scientific proof, providing a voice to the silent remnants imprinted at crime scenes. But the interpretation of such evidence is where the stakes lie. Competent analysis can mean the difference between a just verdict and a miscarriage of justice. The objective lens of forensic science can illuminate truths hidden in the aftermath of crimes, offering a form of clarity unattainable by other means.

Training and education in forensic sciences have evolved to meet these modern demands. Aspiring specialists undergo rigorous coursework and practical exposure to refine their skills. The integration of forensic science into television and literature has fueled public interest and understanding, encouraging young minds to pursue careers in this dynamic domain. It's this blend of passion and precision that propels forensic science forward, ensuring its pivotal role in the complex dance between law and justice.

Intriguingly, forensic science has also filtered into public consciousness through popular media, reshaping the layperson's perception of crime-solving. While dramatizations often stretch the truth—with rapid lab results and conclusive evidence delivered in a one-hour episode—they have nonetheless cemented the importance of science in investigations. This visibility drives both public interest and scrutiny, demanding advancements and accountability within forensic practice.

In conclusion, forensic science in modern investigations is more than just a supporting character in the narrative of criminal justice. It's a central force, a beacon of innovation and renewal, rooted deeply in truth-seeking. With each innovation and each scientific discovery, it reshapes the landscape of crime-solving, offering hope and resolution against humanity's darkest shadows. As it continues to evolve, forensic science stands not only as a witness to history but as an active participant in crafting its future trajectory.

Case Study: Forensic Breakthroughs

In the annals of crime-solving, certain moments stand out as milestones, where methodical persistence met revolutionary technology to not only crack cases but to rewrite the very textbook of forensic science. One such watershed moment occurred with the advent and then the evolution of DNA profiling. This technique didn't just refine forensic science; it fundamentally altered the landscape of criminal investigations worldwide.

Take, for instance, the harrowing case of the " Colin Pitchfork murders." Before DNA fingerprinting, forensic scientists leaned heavily on older methods, such as blood typing, which offered only probabilities rather than certainties. In a twisted turn of events in the mid-1980s, it was DNA profiling that conclusively tied Pitchfork to the murder of two young girls in a quiet village in England. Alec Jeffreys, the scientist behind this groundbreaking methodology, effectively demonstrated the power of genetic fingerprinting. His work shifted a suspect pool of thousands down to one individual, ensuring that science transcended doubt for the first time. The implications of this case were staggering, offering a glimpse into a future where justice could be scientifically validated.

Yet, DNA wasn't the sole champion in this narrative of innovation. Around the same time, advancements in forensic toxicology were making headway in identifying causes of death where trauma wasn't immediately evident. The " Tylenol Murders" of 1982, a case involving cyanide-laced painkillers, sparked a nationwide panic and prompted myriad changes in product packaging and federal anti-tampering laws. The forensic investigators, through painstaking chemical analysis, identified cyanide as the lethally silent perpetrator. Their work underscored the importance of chemical forensics and its ability to provide closure in the most opaque of circumstances.

Building on these breakthroughs, let's not forget the role that trace evidence played in solving the infamous " Unabomber" case. Between 1978 and 1995, Theodore Kaczynski waged a deadly campaign across the United States, eluding law enforcement for years. What finally broke the case open wasn't just a single piece of evidence but a meticulous compilation of forensic findings. Tiny metal fragments, bomb components, and even forensic linguistics contributed to his capture. The investigation highlighted how the synergy of different forensic domains can crack even the most convoluted cases.

One can't discuss forensic breakthroughs without mentioning the Boston Strangler case from the 1960s, which lingered with uncertainty for decades. It wasn't until 2013 that Albert DeSalvo was definitively linked to Mary Sullivan's murder through advances in DNA analysis techniques. Distilling viable DNA from a decades-old crime scene exemplifies forensic science's relentless capability of conjoining the present with the past, ultimately rewriting history.

Another compelling tale of forensic prowess is seen in the use of forensic anthropology. This discipline was famously showcased in the aftermath of the Rwandan genocide. Here, anthropologists meticulously pieced together the remains scattered across various mass graves, ensuring that victims were identified and their stories heard. Each bone, a shapely artifact of birthright and demise, provided compelling testimonies that human atrocities bore reparation through scientific truth.

The field has burgeoned beyond traditional expectations, integrating digital forensics in our increasingly cybernetic world. The " BTK Killer" case brought this to the fore, where Dennis Rader was ensnared partly due to a digital trail. Analysis of a floppy disk, which Rader himself sent to the police thinking it was secure, proved his undoing. This progression underscores a pivotal direction for forensic science in the digital age, a domain where bits and bytes now hold as much weight as physical evidence.

We also see this in the diligent reconstruction of mobile device activity, which played a crucial role in the prosecution of Casey Anthony in 2011. Investigators used cell tower data and GPS findings to weave a narrative that outlined her whereabouts, proving that spatial data could provide as much context as conventional evidence could.

Looking at these cases collectively, it's evident that forensic breakthroughs aren't mere coincidences; they're deliberate evolutions driven by humanity's unyielding quest for truth. These stories weave together a tapestry of scientific progress and human intuition, highlighting how forensic science has continually pushed the boundaries of what was once considered possible.

The future might hold further integration of artificial intelligence, advancements in next-gen sequencing, or novel molecular markers that we can't yet predict. As forensic science marches into the future, these stirring tales of past breakthroughs assure us of one thing: the pursuit of justice will always find new champions in the corridors of science.

Chapter 3:
Analyzing Crime Scenes

At the heart of every criminal investigation lies the crime scene, a silent, telltale witness to the events that unfolded within its confines. This chapter dives into the meticulous and often painstaking process of analyzing these crucial spaces. From the moment investigators arrive, a careful choreography begins, designed to preserve the integrity of the scene. The first responders secure the perimeter, ensuring no evidence inadvertently disappears. As detectives map out the area, each fragment of evidence is cataloged, tagged, and photographed, capturing a moment frozen in time. This environment, though static, speaks volumes; it's up to the keen eyes of seasoned investigators to unravel its narrative. The interplay of light, shadow, and the subtle yet macabre art of trace evidence create a puzzle that demands both patience and precision. By methodically piecing together each element, investigators construct a story that leads them closer to the suspect, turning whispers of the past into a clear, undeniable truth.

Crime Scene Documentation

The process of documenting a crime scene is a meticulous art, where every detail matters. This documentation forms the backbone of a criminal investigation, providing a comprehensive record that investigators can refer to at any point. It's not just about capturing the obvious but also meticulously noting each subtle nuance that could be critical to solving the crime. This section delves into the importance, methods, and challenges of effective crime scene documentation.

Imagine stepping onto a crime scene for the first time. The sense of urgency contrasts sharply with the need for deliberate and methodical recording. Every investigator knows that these initial observations are often critical. In many ways, documenting a crime scene is a race against time; elements change, and fleeting evidence can be lost forever if not promptly captured. Forensic experts work closely with law enforcement officers to ensure that nothing is overlooked, everything from a broken window to a single strand of hair must be noted and preserved.

Photographic evidence is a cornerstone of crime scene documentation. Photographs do more than capture the scene; they provide a visual narrative that can illustrate the progression of a crime. Crime scene photographers utilize high-resolution cameras and, often, video recordings to document every angle of the scene. This serves a dual purpose: preserving a preparatory record for investigators and laying out evidence for potential judicial proceedings. Photographs can become a permanent witness, presenting irrefutable visual testimony.

Field notes are equally important in crime scene documentation. These notes are comprehensive, capturing everything from environmental conditions to initial hypotheses about the crime. Notes must be as detailed and accurate as possible; they often include drawings or sketches that provide a spatial context, which photos alone might not fully convey. It's like weaving a fabric of the crime, where each thread contributes to the whole picture. Essential observations about the scene's layout, time, weather, or even odors, although subjective, can provide future insights to the detectives revisiting the case.

A significant aspect of documentation involves creating a detailed sketch of the crime scene. These sketches are not mere crude drawings but are precise representations of the layout, helping to pinpoint the location of evidence. They're often to scale, providing exact measurements that assist forensic teams when reconstructing the events later on. Such sketches might include position markers for where evidence was found, entry points, and other relevant details crucial for analysis. While they may not have the immediate impact of a photo, their precision and clarity can often reveal aspects of the crime not initially apparent.

Besides visual and written documentation, technological advancements have introduced new layers to crime scene recording. 3D laser scanning technology, for instance, can create detailed digital maps of crime scenes. These scans produce models that offer an immersive perspective, allowing investigators to virtually walk through a scene long after it has been cleared. Such tools enhance the ability to examine multiple aspects of a crime scene, providing invaluable insights into complex cases where spatial relationships are key.

But technology, while opening new doors, also presents challenges. The sheer volume of data generated can be daunting, and ensuring the accuracy of this data requires cross-verification with physical evidence. Moreover, maintaining and protecting this digital evidence against loss or tampering becomes an additional concern, underscoring the need for rigorous protocols in digital evidence management.

Controlling access to a crime scene is paramount to ensuring the integrity of documentation. Every person entering and exiting the scene can potentially alter the physical evidence available, thus detailed logs of such movements are kept. This protocol ensures that any changes to the scene can be accounted for, especially during the chain of custody required for legally admissible evidence.

Clearly, documenting a crime scene isn't just about facts and figures; there's a human element that mustn't be ignored. For investigators, striking a balance between professionalism and empathy can be challenging—particularly in emotionally charged situations. Investigators need to remain detached enough to see the scene objectively, yet sensitive enough to consider any human factors that could have influenced the crime or its subsequent attempt at concealment.

The better the documentation, the stronger the investigation will stand in court. This importance is reflected in the rigorous standards and protocols followed during documentation, all designed to build a case that can withstand scrutiny. Evidence collected and documented must be presented in context, with investigators often needing to articulate how the documentation supports or challenges their theories.

However, errors can still occur, even with the most rigorous care. These mistakes could be as simple as a mislabeled photo or as grave as a contaminated evidence sample. While not every error is fatal to a case, in the high-stakes world of criminal investigation, even small missteps can be magnified in the courtroom. Therefore, documentation is often a collaborative effort, subject to peer reviews and oversight to minimize human error. The checks and balances in place aim to catch errors before they evolve into significant issues that could compromise case integrity.

Documentation at a crime scene indeed sets the stage for the entire investigation. When done well, it tells a story—not just of what happened, but how. It offers clarity amid chaos, a way to piece together truth from a jigsaw of human error, emotion, and evidence. As the bastion of truth in criminal investigations, effective documentation stands as an essential skill that all forensic and law enforcement professionals must master to unravel the often-complicated tapestry of criminal activity.

Evidence Collection Best Practices

In the dim light of a crime scene, precision and attention to detail shine as the guiding stars for investigators. The moment law enforcement professionals cross the threshold of a potential crime site, every tiny detail becomes a crucial puzzle piece. Collecting evidence isn't merely about gathering what's visible; it's about uncovering the hidden narrative locked within each fiber and fingerprint. Understanding how and where to start is foundational to securing justice in any investigation.

Before diving into the particulars, the primary rule stands clear: securing the scene is non-negotiable. This first step ensures that evidence remains untampered, preventing interference from unwarranted personnel. An unprotected site might lead to compromised evidence, which could dilute its efficacy in courtrooms. Officers cordon off areas with tape, establishing boundaries that both shield and maintain the integrity of the evidence trapped within.

Once the area is marked, a systematic approach takes precedence. Investigators embark on a sweeping visual reconnaissance, noting any overt elements aligned or out of place. Documenting these observations through photography or sketching captures the scene's essence before any item is disturbed. Prosecutors and defense attorneys often revisit these records, piecing together timelines and sequences to portray the untainted truth to juries.

Now, let's delve into the evidence itself. Physical evidence—tangible items that can paint a vivid picture of events—ranges from weapons to the most innocuous everyday objects. Each piece needs careful handling. Investigators employ gloves, tweezers, and forceps to ensure that neither contamination nor additional fingerprints mar the findings. Chain of custody documentation starts from the moment an item is collected, an unbroken chronological log of every handler, ensuring the evidence's integrity remains intact.

The biological components—blood, hair, or bodily fluids—play a different game. These samples hold the power of DNA, a microscopic storyteller detailing individual involvement. Such samples demand special storage considerations, often refrigerated, to maintain their viability. Accurately labeled vials and sealed containers await transportation to forensic labs, where science further deciphers the story's complexities.

And we can't ignore trace evidence, the microscopic fragments often overlooked by those with an untrained eye. Fibers, soil, and residues cling to clothing or embed within carpets, revealing unseen interactions or movements. Collecting these requires adept skills and sharp eyes, utilizing tape lifts and vacuum techniques to glean every possible clue. These traces often bind the invisible threads of a story, linking suspect and victim beyond mere acquaintance.

Meanwhile, adherence to protocols and standard operating procedures minimizes discrepancies and errors. Each jurisdiction has its guidelines, but common practices often overlap, derived from years of trial and error. These protocols form a pillar of reassurance, ensuring that even in the high-pressure scenarios of crime scenes, chaos doesn't devour order.

Ethical considerations hold equal weight within this methodology. Officers must maintain a professional demeanor, respecting both victims and suspects while withholding judgment. Evidence must speak for itself, unfettered by bias or preconception. Every item and every absence tells a story, and it's the investigator's duty to narrate it faithfully.

Emerging technologies also augment evidence collection. For instance, alternate light sources (ALS) help detect substances not visible to the naked eye, like invisible inks or body fluids. Enhanced digital forensics tools allow the extraction of data from electronic devices, providing invaluable leads in cases involving cyber elements.

Staying abreast of these advancements positions investigators on the leading edge of effective evidence collection.

Yet, it's not just about the what and the how—it's about the why. Investigators must always ponder what they aim to uncover and how their findings fit within the larger narrative of justice. Is the evidence corroborating or contradicting existing accounts? Each day throws new challenges, reminding those in the field to keep a critical, analytical mindset.

Evidence collection wraps more than just practical know-how; it requires a mentality attuned to minute details and patterns. Investigators are as much artists painting a scene with facts and figures as they are scientists following rigor and methodology. Their craft demands an unyielding balance between adaptability and discipline, right before their entire orchestration finds the stage of a courtroom.

As we continue to peel the layers of what it takes to uncover truths and engineer justice, let's not forget—every piece of evidence is a testament, waiting to hear its voice. Behind the swathes of yellow tape and blinding flash of forensic tools, the dedication to these practices remains the bedrock upon which justice firmly stands.

Chapter 4:
Interrogation and
Interview Techniques

In the dimly-lit rooms where truth becomes elusive, mastering the art of interrogation and interviewing is as crucial as it is intricate. It's a game of psychology, where establishing rapport and reading subtle cues can unearth pivotal truths. Interrogators aren't just asking questions; they're unlocking stories, negotiating with silence, and interpreting every gesture. A successful interrogation can pivot a case towards justice, but the path is fraught with ethical dilemmas and the skillful dance of persuasion versus coercion. Here, the lines blur between instinctive human interaction and disciplined investigative techniques. Crafting the right questions and knowing when to let a suspect's narrative unfold uninterrupted are skills honed over time. This chapter dives into the nuanced strategies that distinguish successful interrogators, who navigate a world where every word and pause holds weight, from the unprepared. It's not just about getting a confession; it's about understanding the human psyche and creating a handshake between truth and justice.

Psychological Approaches in Interrogations

In the realm of criminal investigations, interrogations are pivotal moments. They're where truths are unveiled, stories are woven, and sometimes, confessions are born. The process, however, is more intricate than simply asking questions. The psychological approaches employed during interrogations can make the difference between extracting the truth and hitting a dead end. This segment peels back the layers of these methods, offering insight into the mind games and strategies that can make interrogations effective.

Historically, interrogations were more about endurance than strategy. The conventional methods often leaned heavily on physical presence and intimidation — techniques better suited to coercion than understanding. But the modern era has ushered in a shift towards psychological finesse. The focus now is on understanding the suspect's mental state, motivations, and vulnerabilities. Through empathy and strategic questioning, investigators aim to create an atmosphere conducive to truth-telling.

Interrogation is as much an art as it is a science. At its core lies the Reid Technique, one of the most renowned and widely used psychological approaches globally. Developed in the 1950s, this method integrates various psychological tricks, from the evolved use of empathy to tactical silence. Investigators employing this technique enter the interrogation room not just seeking to ask questions, but hoping to script a confession, carefully guiding a suspect into a narrative where confession becomes the best option.

The Reid Technique unfolds in nine distinct stages, starting with direct confrontation. It's vital that the interrogator demonstrates certainty — not arrogance, but confidence in the suspect's involvement. As the process evolves, the focus shifts to theme development, where investigators craft perceptible narratives around the suspect's alleged involvement, aiding them to rationalize and confess. This psychological weaving does more than accuse; it essentially offers a path to redemption.

Contrasting the rigidity of the Reid Technique, there's another technique gaining traction: the PEACE model, utilized broadly in the United Kingdom and several other countries. The PEACE model stands for Preparation and Planning, Engage and Explain, Account, Closure, and Evaluate. It's built on less accusatory grounds and more on collaboration and transparency. By encouraging open dialogue, the PEACE model aims to gather information without pressure, seeing the suspect as part of the truth-finding process rather than the target of it.

The dichotomy between these techniques raises important questions about morality and efficiency. While the Reid Technique has criticized potential false confessions, the PEACE model strives to reduce these risks through a less confrontational approach.

Understanding these methodologies adds depth to our comprehension of interrogations, but let's not forget the overarching influence of the psychology of language. Skilled interrogators excel in honing their linguistic skills, employing carefully chosen words and controlled tones. Language becomes a tool for weaving webs of trust, subtly nudging the suspect towards cooperation or betrayal of their guarded truths. This dexterity involves knowing when to mirror the suspect's own speech patterns or when to shift into a more assertive vernacular.

Human psychology is nuanced, encompassing an array of emotions and reactions. During an interrogation, attentive detectives focus on more than just the words spoken. Body language — the shifting eyes, fidgeting hands, sudden postural changes — serves as a rich, non-verbal dialogue, often more revealing than the verbal counterpart. For thoroughness, interrogators train to read these cues, piecing together inconsistencies or congruencies that might tip the scales of truth.

The psychological strategies applied in interrogation go beyond the individuals directly involved. Family dynamics, social affiliations, and the suspect's personal history often come into play. An understanding of these aspects can provide crucial leverage, offering interrogators perspectives they might exploit — or respect — to facilitate honesty.

Suspects aren't just criminals in the eyes of those questioning them; they're sons, daughters, partners, friends, each role carrying its unique pressures and expectations that can be tactically addressed during the interrogation.

In crafting a psychological profile of the suspect, investigators often collaborate with psychologists who provide insights into optimal questioning tactics based on the suspect's personality traits. This collaboration can sometimes involve mock interviews and strategic questioning drills. It's a dance of psychological insight channeled through the sharp precision of skilled interrogation—maintaining a balance between too much pressure and too little.

Not just limited to individual suspects, psychological tactics prove significant when multiple actors are questioned. The dynamics shift when dealing with organized crimes, where loyalty might be strong, and fear of retribution palpable. In such scenarios, breaking a suspect's allegiance often requires multifaceted strategies that weave between psychological manipulation and sheer negotiation skills.

Ultimately, psychological approaches in interrogations highlight the human aspect of criminal investigations. They're about understanding the intricate tapestry of human emotion and thought. It's an exercise in patience and strategy where coercion takes a backseat to rapport-building and subtle manipulation. In these interrogative settings, amidst the play of shadows and light, the truth finds its most inadvertent champion: the whisper of the mind slowly unraveling its guarded secrets.

As psychological approaches continue to evolve, they challenge the very fabric of investigative techniques. They emphasize understanding over dominance, persuasion over coercion, and most significantly — the unyielding belief that every human, when approached with the right psychological strategy, has the potential to reveal truths long hidden.

Effective Interview Strategies

In the vast and intricate realm of criminal investigations, interviews often stand as the linchpin, bridging elusive evidence with the quest for truth. Unlike the high-pressure dynamics of an interrogation, interviews tread a more conversational path, seeking to elicit information without overt coercion. They require a detective to don many hats—empathetic listener, keen observer, and strategic questioner—each role crucial in piecing together narratives from fragmented recollections.

Understanding the psychology behind interviews can drastically enhance their effectiveness. While each witness or suspect is unique, human nature's predictability can often be an ally. People tend to respond better when they feel valued and heard. Establishing rapport becomes the pivotal first step. By creating an atmosphere of trust and safety, interviewees are more likely to open up, even inadvertently revealing truths embedded within their subconscious narratives.

Good interview strategies hinge on the art of crafting open-ended questions. These are invitations for the interviewee to narrate freely, rather than confining them to binary yes-or-no responses. A question like " Can you describe the events of that evening in your own words?" encourages expansive discourse. It grants the interviewer insight into not only what happened but also how the interviewee perceives the events.

Utilizing silence is another powerful technique, albeit counterintuitive. In conversation, silences often press individuals to continue speaking, sometimes divulging more than they initially intended. This phenomena occurs because humans naturally seek to fill conversational voids. A strategically placed pause can thus serve as a non-verbal probe, encouraging deeper revelations.

Active listening, meanwhile, cannot be overstated. It's not merely about hearing the words spoken but involves reading between the lines, noting inconsistencies, body language, and other non-verbal cues that complete the communicative tapestry. An astute interviewer pays attention not just to what is said, but also what is left unsaid, picking up on tonal shifts or hesitations that may hint at underlying truths.

The setting of an interview can also significantly impact its outcome. A sterile room adorned with stark fluorescent lighting, reminiscent of a police interrogation room, might inhibit an interviewee's comfort. Conversely, a more casual environment, perhaps with softer lighting and comfortable seating, can diffuse tension and foster a more open dialogue. The aim is to create an atmosphere where the interviewee feels at ease yet aware of the formality of the situation.

Timing plays its part too. If an individual is interviewed too soon after a distressing event, their account may be overwhelmed by emotional upheaval, resulting in a skewed or incomplete version of events. Conversely, waiting too long might lead to details fading into the fog of memory. Striking the right balance is crucial—interviewers must be astutely aware of the mental and emotional state of their subjects.

Technology has also revolutionized interview strategies. Video recording interviews can capture nuances missed by the human eye, allowing for detailed analysis later. However, technology must be wielded judiciously; its presence, if mismanaged, could make interviewees self-conscious. That's where skilled interviewers really shine: balancing human interaction with technological assistance.

Interviews with children or vulnerable individuals demand even greater finesse and specialized approaches. It is critical to ensure that these interviewees aren't retraumatized or unduly influenced by the process. Gentle questioning and a supportive friend-or-family presence, if appropriate, can make these sensitive interviews more effective and ethical.

In the world of criminal investigation, interviews must never be static, one-size-fits-all endeavors. Detectives must mold their strategies to fit the complexities of each case and the intricacies of each mind they probe. They must continuously hone their craft, learning from past successes and missteps to weave an ever-more-effective tapestry of truth finding pursuits.

Recognizing the limitations of an interview is also key. Not every interviewee will provide the silver bullet of a case. Some may be unwilling or genuinely unable to recall critical information. It falls on the adept interviewer to blend patience with persistence, knowing when to push for more detail and when to step back and reassess.

Ultimately, effective interviews come down to a combination of art and science, intuition and technique. They form the backbone of criminal investigations, fleshing out narratives that forensic evidence may not be able to tell on its own. As crime-solving continues to evolve, so too must the methods that detectives employ to engage with the human elements of their investigations.

Chapter 5:
Criminal Profiling

In the complex realm of criminal investigation, profiling stands as both an art and a science, illuminating the behavioral patterns that weave through the dark labyrinths of criminal minds. This chapter delves into the meticulous craft of criminal profiling, where investigators begin to sketch a portrait of the unknown suspect by piecing together disparate bits of evidence and intuition. Fueled by insights into the psychological underpinnings of behavior, profilers seek to predict and thereby prevent future offenses, while sometimes facing skepticism from traditional law enforcement. These profiles, often based on patterns gleaned from past cases, guide the direction of an investigation and narrow down suspect pools, yet they demand a delicate balance between gut instinct and empirical evidence. By walking readers through this complex process, budding detectives gain a deeper understanding of how an effective profile emerges—one that can hold the key to capturing elusive perpetrators and offering a semblance of justice to those affected by crime.

Developing Criminal Profiles

The intricate process of developing criminal profiles often brings to mind a blend of science, intuition, and art. At the heart of this practice is the desire to delve beyond the obvious, to unmask the unseen patterns of behavior that can link seemingly unrelated crimes or predict future actions. Profiling, in essence, is about creating a psychological portrait of the would-be offender, a composite sketch in words that aims to reveal who they are, why they act the way they do, and how they might continue their criminal activities.

The roots of criminal profiling go back to the early attempts at understanding criminal behavior. This technique wasn't always as organized or scientifically grounded as it is today. In its infancy, profiling relied heavily on the instincts and experience of seasoned detectives. These early profiles were often more art than science, and the use of psychological insight was rudimentary at best. But times have certainly changed.

In modern profiling, psychology plays a pivotal role. Profilers today use a combination of empirical research, psychological theories, and forensic evidence to create comprehensive profiles. They consider factors such as childhood experiences, mental health, personality traits, and environmental influences. These elements act as pieces of a puzzle that, when brought together, provide investigators with a clearer picture of a suspect.

One of the key techniques in developing a profile is examining the crime scene. Each crime scene tells a story, and the way a crime is committed can offer significant insights into the offender's psyche. The choice of weapon, the level of organization, the evidence left behind, all these details are scrutinized to understand the who, what, and why of the crime. In many ways, a profiled offender leaves as much of a signature at a crime scene as they do in the commission of the act itself.

Another critical component is victimology, the study of victims. By understanding the victim's relationship to the perpetrator—or lack thereof—profilers can ascertain motive and intent. This knowledge helps narrow down the suspect list, especially when the apparent randomness of a crime turns out to be not so random after all.

Profilers must also consider geographic profiling. This involves analyzing the locations of crimes to predict where an offender might live or operate next. Understanding an offender's spatial patterns can provide insights into their habits, lifestyle, and personality. It's like mapping out their comfort zone, showing the areas where they feel most secure and thus most likely to offend.

Behavioral patterns, too, stand as pillars in the establishment of criminal profiles. Offenders, much like everyone else, have routines and patterns. By identifying these trends, profilers can anticipate their moves, and this can be especially useful in ongoing investigations, providing law enforcement with a proactive edge.

It's vital to mention that despite the utility of profiling, it doesn't produce names or exact identities. Instead, it offers probabilities and generates hypotheses. Profiles help investigators direct their focus, prioritize suspects, and make informed decisions that could lead to apprehension.

Moreover, developing a criminal profile requires teamwork and collaboration. It's not just the profilers who contribute; detectives, forensic scientists, and sometimes even psychologists must work in concert. Communication among these disciplines ensures that profiles are as accurate and useful as possible. A well-rounded team can challenge assumptions, fill in gaps, and create a cohesive narrative.

In examining the historical development of criminal profiling, one can't ignore the influence of notable profiling success stories. These cases highlight profiling's potential when done correctly. They demonstrate how the psychological insights provided by profiles can sometimes succeed where traditional methods falter. However, while these stories serve as beacons of profiling's efficacy, they also underscore the method's limitations and the need for ongoing development and refinement in the field.

As criminal profiling becomes more embedded in modern investigative practices, it also faces challenges. Ethical concerns about labeling and privacy, the risk of stereotyping, and the potential for error must be critically addressed. Profiling is as much a science as it is an art, which means it evolves and adapts. It learns from its mistakes and strives to improve with each case.

The future of criminal profiling looks toward integrating more advanced technologies, such as artificial intelligence and data analytics. These tools offer promising prospects for creating even more robust and precise profiles. By analyzing larger sets of data more quickly than the human mind ever could, technology aims to bolster the profiler's ability to synthesize complex information and uncover insights that may be overlooked otherwise.

Furthermore, profiles are becoming more inclusive of cultural and social factors. Recognizing the diversity of offenders and their backgrounds is essential in developing profiles that accurately reflect the complexities of human behavior. By considering these aspects, profilers aim to create more nuanced and effective profiles that transcend stereotypes and assumptions.

Ultimately, developing criminal profiles is about understanding human behavior at its most fundamental level. It seeks to link seemingly disconnected dots, to provide clarity amidst chaos. Profiling, with its blend of science and intuition, not only aids in apprehending offenders but also in preventing future crimes. As the criminal world becomes more complex, so too must the techniques used to combat it, ensuring that justice, though at times elusive, remains always within reach.

Case Example: Profiling Success Stories

The art of criminal profiling lies in its unique ability to construct a psychological and behavioral sketch of suspects, leading to breakthroughs in even the most perplexing cases. Let's delve into some notable examples where profiling played a pivotal role in solving crimes, illustrating its importance and efficacy in the investigative process.

The case of the " Mad Bomber" in New York City during the mid-20th century stands as one of the earliest and most celebrated successes in criminal profiling history. Over a span of 16 years, a series of bombings occurred across the city, terrorizing the public and eluding law enforcement. It was the profile created by Dr. James Brussel, a pioneering psychiatrist, that led to the capture of George Metesky. Brussel's meticulous profile included details as specific as the bomber's probable attire upon arrest, and remarkably, Metesky was wearing exactly what Brussel had predicted. This case marked a turning point, showcasing profiling as a valuable tool in criminal investigations.

Moving forward several decades, the investigation into the " Green River Killer" case illustrates how profiling adapts and refines its techniques over time. In the 1980s, a string of murders along Washington's Green River remained unsolved for years. Profilers worked tirelessly to identify patterns and psychological markers, understanding that the killer might be operating within a certain comfort zone and possibly masking homicidal tendencies behind a façade of normalcy. This profile directed police to focus on certain suspects, eventually leading to the arrest of Gary Ridgway. The blend of profiling with forensic advances such as DNA analysis was essential in confirming Ridgway as the perpetrator.

Then there is the case of Ted Bundy, one of America's most notorious serial killers. Bundy's ability to charm and deceive victims and the authorities alike made him a particularly challenging suspect to apprehend. However, it was the work of dedicated profilers who recognized the distinct patterns in his killing spree—the geographical foci, the choice of victims, and the timespan between killings—that provided insight into Bundy's pathological behavior. Profilers were able to predict his movements and narrow down potential next targets, contributing significantly to his eventual capture.

Profiling's contribution to solving the BTK (Bind, Torture, Kill) murders in Wichita, Kansas, also serves as a testament to its potency. Dennis Rader, the BTK killer, eluded capture for decades, leaving a trail of communications that taunted investigators. It was through careful analysis of Rader's written communications and the psychological signature they contained that profilers were able to develop a clear understanding of his personality traits and potential weaknesses. This understanding was crucial when Rader eventually tripped up by providing clues that led to his downfall.

Another success story stems from the case of the Unabomber, Ted Kaczynski. The investigation's turning point came when the FBI Behavioral Analysis Unit applied profiling techniques to Kaczynski's manifesto. By deciphering the language and underlying messages, profilers were able to infer a great deal about the personality and motivations of the Unabomber. When Kaczynski's brother recognized these traits, it led directly to Kaczynski's arrest, underscoring how profiling does not just aid in identifying " who" but also " why" .

Not all profiling success stories are high-profile cases. In numerous lesser-known instances, criminal profiling has quietly guided investigations by narrowing down suspect lists and focusing investigative efforts. In one such case, a spree of burglaries that escalated to physical attacks stumped a small-town police force. Profilers considered the offender's method and timing, identifying a pattern that led to the apprehension of a suspect previously uninvolved in any investigations. These everyday successes highlight profiling as an indispensable instrument beyond the celebrated accounts.

Criminal profiling isn't just reactive; it's increasingly being used in proactive measures. By analyzing profiles of past offenders and understanding the triggers that lead to criminal behavior, law enforcement agencies can potentially prevent crimes by identifying warning signs in at-risk individuals. This approach is being integrated with community policing efforts to identify potential threats before they manifest.

The success of criminal profiling in these cases isn't merely a testament to individual genius but rather a reflection of a disciplined approach that combines behavioral science, meticulous observation, and a deep understanding of human nature. These methodologies have now become integral to how complex investigations are conducted and solved, reinforcing the value of profiling as a cornerstone of modern criminology.

The tales of profiling success offer rich lessons in intuition and logic, highlighting the role of experience and insight over a reliance on solely technological means. As criminal minds evolve, so too will profiling, continuously adapting to rise with new challenges. It's not just about catching the criminal; it's about understanding them in a way that helps protect future victims.

While criminal profiling continues to face skepticism and debate, especially in legal circles, its place in the broader framework of criminal investigation is undeniably significant. When combined effectively with forensic evidence and traditional detective work, profiling acts as a catalyst for solving even the most enigmatic crimes.

In summary, the success stories of criminal profiling are testament to its power and utility. These narratives not only kindle the imagination but also drive home the importance of understanding the criminal psyche. They demonstrate how, with a mix of science and intuition, detectives can unveil disturbing truths from the shadows of human behavior, making the intricate dance of crime-solving a little more comprehensible for us all.

Chapter 6:
The Art of Surveillance

In the world of criminal investigation, surveillance emerges as both an art and a science, one where patience, precision, and technology intertwine to unlock the hidden narratives of a suspect's life. Investigators transform into shadowy figures, mastering the craft of remaining unseen while capturing the tiniest details that may elude an untrained eye. It's a delicate dance, utilizing everything from high-tech gadgets to the humble notepad, where success hinges on strategy and timing. Surveillance demands a keen understanding of human behavior, predicting movements and anticipating the unexpected. Even in this covert realm, ethical lines bind detectives, challenging them to balance the need for information with respect for privacy. Thus, navigating the complex terrain of surveillance becomes a crucial skill, sharpening detectives' ability to see without being seen.

Tools and Technology in Surveillance

In the tapestry of criminal investigation, few threads are as complex and pivotal as those of surveillance. The art of surveillance, more than a mere observational tactic, embraces a myriad of sophisticated tools and cutting-edge technologies that have evolved substantially over the decades. These devices and methodologies are central to unraveling cases that once eluded even the sharpest of detectives. So, what are these tools, and how do they facilitate the delicate dance of watching without being seen?

The foundation of modern surveillance lies in the humble yet indispensable piece of equipment: the camera. Today's surveillance cameras sprout far beyond the rudimentary lenses of yesteryear. High-definition cameras, some no larger than a button, have become silent partners in catching illicit activities. They're omnipresent in public places and private spaces alike, eyes that never tire nor blink. Capable of zooming in with precision or capturing an entire landscape, these cameras gather footage used for real-time tracking or retrospective analysis.

The next evolution in surveillance technology takes form as drone systems. Once perceived only in contexts of military or espionage, drones now play a role in the domestic landscape of crime-solving. These aerial marvels provide vantage points inaccessible by human investigators, streaming live footage from above and offering a new perspective on the world below. Their quiet yet assertive presence is a game-changer in cases needing a bird's-eye view.

Let's not overlook the paradigm shift brought about by GPS tracking devices. Relinquishing the need for tailing targets physically, modern investigators can now rely on these compact devices to mark the movements of suspects. Plant a GPS tracker on a suspect's vehicle, and you create a digital breadcrumb trail, meticulously documenting every turn, stop, and detour. It's as close to omnipresence as an investigator might imagine.

Electronic surveillance encompasses more than just visual monitoring. Audio surveillance, bugging devices to the layperson, plays its own critical role. These tiny instruments can be secreted away in places where human ears cannot intrude, capturing snippets of conversation that might prove crucial. Despite their contribution, ethical and legal landscapes surrounding audio surveillance are as intricate as the devices themselves.

In what may seem like a chapter plucked straight out of science fiction, facial recognition software has surfaced as a formidable ally in the surveillance toolkit. Integrating artificial intelligence with computer vision, this software identifies and tracks individuals based on facial features. Airports, city streets, and even retail locales increasingly lean on this tech to recognize known individuals or persons of interest.

Data mining and social media analysis join the ranks of indispensable tools in digital surveillance. In today's hyper-connected environment, individuals leave behind digital footprints across a variety of platforms. Advanced algorithms parse through vast amounts of online data, identifying patterns and connections that may not be visible to the naked eye. Social media content can reveal relationships, locations, and behaviors previously shrouded.

Among the technological marvels, let's not underestimate the role of cybersecurity tools in safeguarding and monitoring digital spaces. Cybercriminals veer between the virtual and physical worlds, warranting the deployment of digital surveillance measures. Tools robust enough to decrypt, analyze, and monitor cyber communications are at the forefront of thwarting digital threats. In a world where data is as valuable as gold, the digital domain demands vigilant oversight.

Of course, employing these advanced tools isn't without challenges. Investigators must navigate a labyrinth of ethical and privacy concerns when deploying surveillance technology. Balancing the need for information with respect for civil liberties remains a contentious issue and is a subject covered in the subsequent section. Often, the legitimacy of surveillance hinges on the nature of warrants and permits, intricate steps that must be negotiated meticulously.

Complex as they are, tools and technology in surveillance continue to adapt and push the boundaries of what's achievable in the fight against crime. In every elusive shadow or whispered conversation, lurking behind each of these is a technological guardian, ready to help justice inch closer to the truth. The art of surveillance is an ongoing materia medica, ever-refining its techniques to keep pace with crafty and sophisticated adversaries, truly embodying the phrase: where there's a will, there's a way.

This dimension of investigation, driven by innovation, heralds a realm where limitations are constantly challenged, promising an era where what was once considered beyond reach now lingers within the grasp of the vigilant investigator.

Ethical Considerations in Surveillance

Surveillance has long been a cornerstone of investigative work, providing critical insights and evidence in the pursuit of justice. However, it also treads on a delicate path marked by ethical challenges and moral dilemmas. At the heart of these considerations lies the balance between privacy and the need for security. When investigators engage in surveillance, they often face the difficult task of navigating personal privacy rights and the public's expectation for safety. These two ideals can be at odds, creating a gray area that requires careful navigation.

From a historical perspective, surveillance has evolved tremendously. With the advent of technology, it has become more sophisticated and pervasive, amplifying its ethical implications. In the past, physical stakeouts and tailing were the primary methods employed by detectives. Today, digital tools like GPS tracking, high-resolution cameras, and online monitoring have transformed how surveillance is conducted. As these tools become more advanced, the line between ethical and unethical surveillance becomes increasingly blurred.

Privacy, a fundamental human right, often collides with surveillance practices. The question arises: how much privacy should individuals be willing to forfeit for the sake of public safety? This is not just a philosophical debate but a practical concern for detectives and law enforcement agencies. In democratic societies, surveillance needs to be justified with probable cause and monitored by legal frameworks to prevent abuse. But even with these safeguards, there remains a risk of overreach, where the quest for information infringes on personal freedoms.

The ethical considerations extend to the technology itself. With tools capable of facial recognition, real-time location tracking, and even predicting behavior, the potential for misuse is significant. These technologies can inadvertently target marginalized communities, exacerbate biases, or be used beyond their intended scope. Investigators and agencies must therefore exercise discretion, using surveillance as a tool for truth and justice, not a blanket method of scrutiny.

Furthermore, transparency and accountability are vital in maintaining ethical standards in surveillance. Members of the public need to trust that surveillance is deployed responsibly and that their rights are protected. Clear policies and oversight mechanisms can help to build this trust. Law enforcement agencies are often required to justify their use of surveillance in courts, providing an essential check against potential abuses. However, the clandestine nature of surveillance often means that such scrutiny is difficult to achieve in practice.

Ethics in surveillance also encompasses the psychological and social impact on those being observed. The knowledge or even suspicion of being watched can alter behavior, erode trust, and lead to a heightened sense of anxiety or paranoia. For communities that are disproportionately monitored, it can foster a sense of disenfranchisement and exacerbate tensions with law enforcement.

Understanding these psychological impacts is crucial for investigators, who must weigh the benefits of surveillance against the potential harm it could cause to the social fabric.

As surveillance becomes more intertwined with technology, ethical training for those involved in its application becomes imperative. Detectives, investigators, and even private companies that develop surveillance technology need to be aware of the moral dimensions of their work. Familiarity with legal guidelines is important, but understanding the broader ethical implications of surveillance can help ensure that it is used in a manner that is just and fair.

Ethical surveillance isn't solely about what is legally permissible but also about what is morally justifiable. Investigators often face split-second decisions and must regularly assess whether their actions align with both the letter of the law and the ethical principles that guide their profession. This reflective practice is essential, especially in cases where the surveillance targets are vulnerable or involve sensitive information.

Moreover, public opinion plays a significant role in shaping the ethical landscape of surveillance. In recent years, high-profile cases and revelations about government and corporate surveillance activities have sparked widespread debate. These discussions often revolve around consent and knowledge—do individuals know they are being surveilled, and have they consented to it, either explicitly or implicitly? The answers to these questions can have profound implications for public trust and the legitimacy of surveillance methods.

Ultimately, the ethical considerations in surveillance require a multifaceted approach. It's a dynamic equilibrium of rights and responsibilities, of ensuring safety while respecting individual freedoms. As surveillance continues to be an integral part of criminal investigation, the commitment to ethical practices remains paramount.

This commitment ensures that while technology may evolve, the dignity and rights of individuals remain safeguarded.

Chapter 7:
The Legal Framework

In the intricate tapestry of criminal investigation, the legal framework forms a foundational thread that guides every action and decision. The convergence of law and investigation demands a precise yet flexible understanding of the judicial system, where each nuance can influence the outcome of a case. The legal process, with its labyrinthine procedures and protocols, ensures that justice isn't just pursued but is attained with integrity. Navigating legal challenges often requires investigators to balance the scales of justice with the demands of their pursuit; it's where the pressure to solve crimes swiftly collides with the necessity for due process. Legal constraints serve as both boundaries and guides, shaping investigative strategies while safeguarding the rights of all involved. In this dynamic interplay, the investigator's knowledge of the legal terrain can mean the difference between a solved mystery and a perpetual enigma, emphasizing the crucial role that legal acumen plays in the realm of criminal investigation.

Understanding the Legal Process

The legal process in criminal investigation serves as both a guide and a hurdle, meticulously outlining the pathway to justice. It's a labyrinthine system where understanding the interplay between law enforcement and the judiciary is crucial. Without this knowledge, efforts to solve crimes and administer justice can falter, sometimes fatally. For those invested in unearthing truths and solving crimes, getting acquainted with this legal dance is non-negotiable.

At the heart of any criminal investigation is the search for truth. But truth must align with procedural laws that govern evidence gathering, suspect rights, and courtroom presentations. These rules exist to ensure fairness and accuracy, preventing miscarriages of justice while balancing the scales of investigating and prosecuting crime. It can seem like a tightrope walk: one wrong step and a case, no matter how airtight, could unravel in front of a judge and jury.

The process typically kicks off with the investigation itself, initiated after a crime report or discovery. Investigators collect evidence, conduct interviews, and follow leads. Yet, every action taken is underpinned by strict legal protocols. Warrants often need procuring for searching premises or seizing evidence. Here, the importance of probable cause – a fundamental legal standard – comes into play. It ensures investigations have a solid foundation before encroaching on individual rights.

Moving forward, the legal process involves critical steps like arrests and arraignments. Arresting a suspect is not simply about apprehending an individual suspected of a crime. It requires adherence to protocols like the Miranda rights – a constitutional protection against self-incrimination, ensuring that suspects are aware of their rights during detention. Failure to properly administer these rights can lead to evidence being inadmissible in court, directly impacting the trajectory of a case.

Once a suspect is in custody, the clock starts ticking. Prosecutors face the task of filing charges within a specified time, governed by the principles of due process. They assess the gathered evidence, determining whether it supports moving forward to trial. This decision marks one of the most pivotal moments in a case, often requiring a careful balancing act between legal sufficiency and public interest.

Plea bargaining enters the picture here as an often-used tool, especially in cases where evidence is overwhelming against the defendant. While some perceive it as a means to achieve quicker resolutions, others see it as forsaking the full pursuit of justice. The implications of plea deals are complex, serving to ease the court's load yet potentially swaying public confidence in the justice system.

As cases progress to trial, the courtroom becomes the theater for legal minds to present arguments, cross-examine witnesses, and introduce evidence. Here, the rules of evidence stand as gatekeepers. They determine what can be shown or stated before a jury, prioritizing relevance and reliability while excluding prejudicial or misleading information. It's a battleground of strategy, where both prosecution and defense ensure that their narratives sway the jury's perspective.

Judges have roles that oscillate between mere arbiters of law and active participants in the courtroom drama. Precedents, jury instructions, and verdict deliveries all rest on their shoulders. Their interpretations of the law can set foundational shifts, reinforcing the importance of judicial discretion within the legal process. Meanwhile, jurors are tasked with absorbing complex legal arguments, ultimately delivering verdicts based on the evidence presented.

Sentencing, should a verdict of guilt be ascertained, follows as a culmination of the legal process. It's where justice takes tangible form, influenced by statutory guidelines, precedents, and the specifics of each case. These decisions weigh heavily, often scrutinized by the public, eager to see justice served in a way they deem fitting.

Appeals provide a recourse for perceived miscarriages of justice. They ensure checks and balances, allowing higher courts to review lower court decisions for legal errors. This aspect of the process emphasizes how the legal system remains dynamic, constantly evolving through interpretations and reconsiderations of established laws.

Understanding the legal process is key for anyone diving into the world of crime-solving. It forms the spine of any investigation, shaping how detectives, lawyers, and judges bring a case from the shadows of doubt to the enlightening corridors of justice. Each step, each decision, echoes with profound significance, culminating in verdicts that speak to the heart of society's quest for truth.

Navigating Legal Challenges in Investigations

Legal challenges are an inevitable part of criminal investigations, weaving a complex web around the pursuit of justice. As detectives embark on the arduous journey of piecing together puzzles of crime, their path is often fraught with legal obstacles. These might seem daunting, especially to those aspiring to step into the shoes of real-life detectives. Yet, navigating this legal labyrinth is just as critical as any forensic breakthrough or psychological profiling, ensuring the investigations not only reach a conclusion but also withstand the rigorous scrutiny of the legal system.

At the heart of these challenges lies the fundamental principle of legal rights—of both victims and suspects. Investigators must tread carefully, respecting constitutional guarantees such as the right to privacy and protection against unlawful search and seizure as outlined in the Fourth Amendment. When gathering evidence, it's paramount they obtain warrants properly; any misstep here, and crucial evidence could be rendered inadmissible. Cases have crumbled in courts over such technicalities, turning seemingly foolproof investigations into lessons etched in caution.

Consider, for instance, the infamous fruit of the poisonous tree doctrine. This legal metaphor warns that evidence obtained through illegal searches or interrogations contaminates subsequent discoveries.

Detectives must therefore ensure that their procedural steps are beyond reproach. It is a delicate balance between thorough investigation and constitutional adherence, where the ladder to justice never justifies overstepping legal bounds. A prime example is the landmark 1961 Supreme Court case, Mapp v. Ohio, which reaffirmed that unlawfully seized evidence cannot be used in state criminal prosecutions, underscoring the necessity of adherence to the law during investigations.

Moreover, detectives often face the intricacies of suspect rights during interrogations. The Miranda warning serves as a crucial touchstone here, reminding investigators of the necessity to inform suspects of their rights to remain silent and have an attorney present. This isn't merely procedural boilerplate; failure to administer these warnings can lead to a suspect's statement being inadmissible, toppling critical parts of the prosecution's case. The timing and manner of issuing the Miranda rights play a decisive role, with entire confessions crumbling to dust if not properly handled.

As detectives maneuver through investigations, the chain of custody is another formidable challenge. This rigorous documentation ensures that evidence remains untampered from the crime scene to the courtroom. Any break in this chain might cast doubt on the evidence's integrity, providing defense attorneys with ammunition to question its validity. This meticulous record-keeping isn't just an administrative task but a foundational aspect of maintaining the credibility of the evidence presented in court.

Adding another layer of complexity is the issue of jurisdiction. Crimes often spill over geographical boundaries, involving multiple law enforcement agencies, each governed by different laws and procedures. Here, inter-agency cooperation is vital but can be mired in bureaucratic red tape. Jurisdictional disputes can delay investigations, presenting another hurdle detectives must clear to keep the momentum of an investigation moving forward. Coordination with federal agencies like the FBI and international bodies is crucial when crimes cross state lines or international borders.

Furthermore, the introduction of technology in investigations carries its own legal nuances. The rise of digital evidence—from emails and social media interactions to encrypted messaging—requires investigators to possess an understanding of cyber law and the etiquette of digital evidence collection. Legal boundaries must guide the acquisition of digital information, as privacy laws and data protection regulations vary greatly, adding another layer of complexity. The era of hacking for evidence is long gone, as courts view such practices as serious violations, often leading to evidence dismissal.

Even the most compelling evidence does little good if it can't be presented in court. This is where the rules of evidence come into play, necessitating an interplay of legal acumen and investigative skill. From understanding the Federal Rules of Evidence to navigating state-specific guidelines, detectives must be attuned to how—and what—evidence can be introduced during trials. It's not just about gathering facts but weaving them into a compelling narrative that aligns with legal standards.

Consider cases where investigators have had to confront legal challenges related to new forensic methods. Cutting-edge technology, like DNA analysis or sophisticated computer algorithms, sometimes finds itself the center of legal scrutiny. Defense lawyers may contest the reliability of such evidence, urging the court to reject its inclusion. Hence, detectives must work closely with forensic experts to ensure that these new methodologies are presented in a way that withstands legal challenges.

While legal frameworks present hurdles, they serve as the bedrock of a just society. Rather than viewing these challenges as impediments, detectives can see them as guiding forces, ensuring the moral compass of an investigation remains true. Navigating these legal intricacies doesn't just make one a better detective but fortifies the very pursuit of justice. It calls for a deep understanding of both the law and the human elements within it, a synergy that transforms the investigative process into a disciplined craft.

For budding investigators, understanding these legal landscapes is crucial. Real-life crime-solving is far more intricate than the fiction it often inspires. It demands not only deduction and perseverance but also a rigorous respect for the rule of law. The dance between investigation and legal procedure is delicate—each step matters, and each misstep could lead to significant setbacks.

Chapter 8:
Cold Cases and Unsolved Mysteries

In the shadowy realm of unsolved mysteries, time seems to stand still, leaving victims' voices trapped in the corridors of history, whispering for justice. As investigations stall or grow cold, the relentless pursuit for answers is rekindled by technological advances and fresh perspectives. Detectives today, armed with new tools and strategies, confront these haunting puzzles not as remnants of the past but as challenges begging for modern solutions. Reopening cold cases isn't just about dusty files and forgotten evidence; it's a meticulous dance with the past, balancing intuition and science. By revisiting famous cases, investigators offer hope for closure, unearthing truths that can finally offer solace to those who've waited too long. In this intricate dance, each step could lead to revelations or lead further into the labyrinth of mystery.

Strategies for Reopening Cold Cases

Cold cases, often shrouded in mystery and silence, captivate the minds of true crime enthusiasts and aspiring detectives alike. Opening these dormant files isn't merely a return to dusty archives; it's a quest to find justice long delayed. The process involves a meticulous approach, combining old-fashioned detective work with modern innovation.

One paramount strategy is to make use of advances in forensic science. It's astounding how much information can remain preserved on biological evidence, waiting patiently for the right technology to expose secrets once thought buried. DNA analysis, in particular, has revolutionized cold case investigations. Old evidence kits revisited with today's techniques can yield results that were unimaginable when the cases first hit a dead end.

The re-examination of evidence extends beyond biological materials. Technological prowess has made it possible to enhance and scrutinize video and audio recordings in ways formerly impossible. Historical fingerprint techniques, too, have advanced, allowing investigators to run prints through updated databases, often yielding new leads. It's not just the hidden that's revealed, but the overlooked.

Despite technological advances, a human element remains indispensable. Many cases benefit from a fresh set of eyes—an investigator unburdened by the assumptions and pressures of the original team. These 'cold case squads' approach files with a mix of skepticism and curiosity, questioning everything with a dogged determination.

Interviewing witnesses and those involved is another critical angle. With the passage of time, allegiances change, memories clear up, and guilt gnaws. People might be more willing to divulge crucial pieces of information, knowing that the immediate dangers and stigmas they once faced have diminished. Engaging with potential informants via updated psychological approaches can yield invaluable insights.

Additionally, developing a comprehensive timeline is imperative, as it helps to untangle the myriad events surrounding the case. This timeline acts as a backbone, supporting further investigation and highlighting areas that could stand reinvestigation. Such a chronological framework often illuminates inconsistencies or gaps that require a closer look or new examination techniques.

The role of media should not be underestimated. Re-engaging public interest through media coverage can bring new data and potential witnesses into play. It's a double-edged sword, though, as public attention can also distort perceptions. A carefully balanced media strategy can reignite hope and coax out silent voices.

When it comes to the public and familial interest, collaboration can be key. Often, victims' families have pursued fragments of justice independently for years and may hold scraps of information gleaned from informal networks or private investigations. Working with these stakeholders can sometimes provide pivotal contributions to an investigation's progress. Their insight, raw and emotive, should not be underestimated.

Lastly, international cooperation can prove crucial, especially in cases involving cross-border crimes or suspects who've fled jurisdictions. The development of international databases and cooperation initiatives allows law enforcement to access resources and intelligence previously out of reach.

Solving a cold case is like assembling a puzzle with missing pieces. New pieces occasionally surface, often through unorthodox means, and each can bring clarity to the chaotic picture. It's a complex dance of patience and action, of gathering intelligence and piecing together narratives.

Reopening cold cases requires an open mindset—a willingness to challenge past certainties while embracing innovative methodologies. This blending of the old with the new, backed by determined sleuths and cutting-edge technology, ignites the fight for justice past its sell-by date. In doing so, they remind us that stories, much like justice, deserve to see the light of day.

Famous Cold Cases Revisited

In the labyrinth of unresolved mysteries, some cases stand as silent testimonies to time's passage and the relentless quest for justice. Cold cases are more than just unsolved puzzles; they hold stories waiting to be uncovered, offering glimpses into the darker sides of human nature and the persistent drive of those who seek the truth against all odds. From the Mord in Limehouse to the infamous Zodiac Killer, revisiting these stories isn't merely about recounting grisly details—it's about the hope that one day, justice will prevail.

Take, for instance, the case of the Black Dahlia, a name that still echoes with mystery and horror. In 1947, Elizabeth Short was found brutally murdered in Los Angeles, the crime scene more a tableau of macabre art than anything many had ever witnessed. The investigation was around thirty detectives working round-the-clock, yet they were thwarted by misleading media narratives and a plethora of false confessions. Despite numerous suspects and endless theories, the brutal murder remains unsolved. It's a tale that encapsulates the intersection of sensationalism, despair, and the ceaseless quest for answers in cold cases.

Another haunting enigma is the case of the Zodiac Killer, who terrorized Northern California in the late 1960s and early 1970s. With taunting letters and cryptograms sent to police and newspapers, the Zodiac Killer not only eluded capture but also mocked those who hunted him. While it's tantalizing for true crime aficionados that some of his ciphers were cracked decades later, the identity of the killer remains just out of reach. The Zodiac case illustrates the challenges inherent in cold cases—shifting technology, witness attrition, and the fading memories of those involved—all adding layers of complexity for investigators hoping to finally close the book.

The mysterious disappearance of Jimmy Hoffa, the once powerful labor leader, provides a different lens on cold cases—one entwined with organized crime and power struggles. Hoffa vanished in 1975, last seen outside a Detroit restaurant. Despite countless theories ranging from being entombed in concrete to resting near the shores of the

Great Lakes, his fate remains one of America's most captivating mysteries.

The case's persistence speaks volumes about the powerful forces at play and the shadows that vast networks of influence can cast over justice, rendering some cold cases seemingly unresolvable.

Even more contemporary cold cases hold the public's fascination, especially with the advent of new technologies that seem on the verge of breakthroughs. The 1996 murder of JonBenét Ramsey, a child beauty queen, is a chilling reminder of how fame and innocence can collide tragically. Despite advanced forensic methods and intense public scrutiny, the mystery remains, serving as a catalyst for ongoing debates around investigative practices and the enduring influence of media narratives.

When revisiting cold cases, it's crucial to appreciate the integration of old-school detective work with contemporary technological advances. Consider the Golden State Killer, once a shadow known only by his heinous crimes across California in the 1970s and 80s. His case lay dormant until genetic genealogy—a groundbreaking fusion of forensics and family trees—breathed new life into the investigation. Joseph James DeAngelo's arrest in 2018 showcased the potential latent within cold cases and provided a beacon of hope for others longing to crack similarly stubborn mysteries.

Of course, the lingering allure of these cases is not solely due to their unsolved nature; it's also about the survivors, families, and investigators whose lives have been defined by the pursuit of resolution. These stories serve as a complex tapestry of ongoing detective work, requiring a meticulous piecing together of scant evidence and the human instinct to right the wrongs of the past.

As we weave through these ghostly tales, it's apparent that the path towards unraveling cold cases is neither straightforward nor predictable. It demands perseverance, creativity, and sometimes a touch of serendipity. Each case we revisit in this section is not just a mystery waiting to be solved; it's a reminder of the indomitable spirit of those who refuse to let the past fade into obscurity. As techniques advance and fresh perspectives invigorate old investigations, there's a renewed optimism that someday these mysteries will transition from unsolved legends to closed chapters. Cold cases are an eternal testament to humanity's relentless pursuit of truth, illustrating that no matter how old the trail, there's always the possibility of justice, sometimes when we least expect it.

Chapter 9:
The Impact of Technology

In the modern landscape of criminal investigation, technology stands as both a crucial ally and a formidable challenger, reshaping traditional methods and introducing new frontiers. The digital age has propelled the inception of techniques like digital forensics, where investigators sift through vast troves of data to uncover elusive clues. Every digital footprint tells a story, from encrypted communications to the nuanced trails left on social media. Yet, as rapidly as investigators adapt, perpetrators evolve, employing technology to devise sophisticated cybercrimes that transcend geographical boundaries. This cat-and-mouse game has pushed the boundaries of what's possible, demanding that today's investigators be as technologically savvy as they are intuitively sharp. As future trends emerge, integrating artificial intelligence and advanced data analytics promises to unlock even more secrets from the tangled web of crime. Investigators must, therefore, balance embracing these innovations while remaining ever cautious of their implications, knowing that with each technological step forward comes new ethical and logistical challenges.

Digital Forensics and Cyber Crime

As technology evolves at a breakneck pace, so too does the landscape of criminal activity. The digital age has transformed crime, spawning new forms of illegal activity that stretch the capabilities of traditional law enforcement. Enter digital forensics—a field that plays a crucial role in modern crime-solving. It's a science dedicated to the recovery and investigation of material found in digital devices, often used to uncover evidence that was once thought hidden forever.

At its core, digital forensics is about piecing together electronic puzzles. Whether it's recovering deleted emails, tracing stolen funds through the complex web of the internet, or identifying the source of a malicious hacking attempt, digital forensic experts apply both technical know-how and investigative ingenuity. Their work is as meticulous as it is vital, often forming the backbone of cyber crime investigations by providing tangible evidence that can be used in court.

Cyber crime, a term that covers a multitude of illicit activities occurring primarily online, ranges from identity theft and cyberbullying to more sophisticated operations like corporate espionage and cyber terrorism. Hackers and cyber criminals are often steps ahead, exploiting vulnerabilities with speed and precision. This ongoing cat-and-mouse game requires digital forensic analysts to be equally agile, ready to counter those threats with creative solutions and technical wizardry.

Consider the prevalence of smartphones and personal computers. These devices, while essential in today's world, can also serve as the primary tools for committing crimes. Forensic experts must approach each device with an investigator's mind, examining metadata, timestamps, and even seemingly innocuous user behavior for clues. It's a complex dance of science and art where every file, log, and obscure line of code can signify a breakthrough.

The impact of digital forensics extends beyond the confines of individual cases. In an interconnected world, criminal activity often involves multiple jurisdictions, sometimes leading forensic specialists to collaborate on a global scale. International cooperation becomes critical in tackling issues like human trafficking rings, global fraud operations, and international hacking syndicates. These collaborations require not just technical expertise but also an understanding of diverse legal frameworks and cultural contexts.

One notable example of digital forensics in action is the investigation into ransomware attacks. These attacks often involve malicious software that encrypts a victim's data, with the perpetrator demanding payment for the decryption key. Forensic experts must often decode this piracy, tracing digital breadcrumbs back to the source and, where possible, recovering lost data without giving in to ransom demands. These efforts help law enforcement agencies dismantle ransomware networks and bring offenders to justice.

The importance of digital forensics is also underscored in the realm of cybersecurity. By analyzing breach tactics, forensic experts not only help solve crimes but also contribute to developing better defenses against future attacks. Security protocols and software are regularly updated based on the findings of these investigations, making our digital spaces safer for all.

Indeed, the challenges are significant. Digital forensics must keep pace with the fast-moving environment of technological advancement. Encrypted communications, anonymizing technologies like VPNs and Tor, and the burgeoning field of cryptocurrencies represent new hurdles. These innovations, while beneficial for personal privacy, can also be used to disguise criminal activity, requiring forensic teams to innovate constantly.

Despite these challenges, the field continues to make strides. Tools are becoming more sophisticated and user-friendly, enabling wider access for law enforcement agencies. Automated systems can now sort through vast opportunities of data to highlight relevant pieces for investigators. This automation allows experts to focus on analysis, strategizing solutions, and less on the initial data crunching.

Educational programs and certifications in digital forensics have proliferated too. Universities and professional bodies offer courses designed to build a skilled workforce ready to meet the demands of digital crime-solving. These courses cover everything from the basics of network security to the complexities of cloud-based investigations, ensuring a new generation of forensic experts is ready to tackle whatever challenges the future holds.

The story of digital forensics is one of innovation in the face of adversity. It's a field that requires not just technical skills but also a dedication to understanding the human elements behind digital trails. Cyber crime will continue to evolve, but with the aid of digital forensics, law enforcement has a fighting chance to stay one step ahead. The impact of technology on crime-solving is profound, and as we look to the future, the role of digital forensics will only become more pivotal in our endeavor to uphold justice in the shadowy world of cyber crime.

Future Trends in Criminal Investigation

As technology reshapes the world at an accelerating pace, the landscape of criminal investigation is no exception to this transformation. The intersection of cutting-edge advancements and investigative techniques promises to revolutionize how crimes are solved in the years to come. Imagine a world where the clues left behind at a crime scene are deciphered instantaneously, where digital fingerprints are rendered as clear as physical ones, and where interconnected data streams map out the movements and motives of suspects with pinpoint accuracy. To truly grasp what's on the horizon for criminal investigations, it's essential to delve into the technologies and approaches that are poised to lead this next generation of crime-solving.

Consider artificial intelligence (AI) and machine learning, two fields that are already making significant inroads into criminal investigations. These technologies are expected to become even more sophisticated in predicting criminal activity and aiding law enforcement agencies in piecing together intricate crime scenarios. AI can sift through enormous datasets at lightning speed, identifying patterns and anomalies that a human eye might miss. With machine learning, these systems can constantly improve, enhancing their ability to forecast where and when crimes might occur and even suggesting likely suspects based on previous patterns. This predictive capacity is revolutionary; it means acting before a crime is committed or catching the criminal faster than ever before.

Virtual and augmented reality also promise to redefine how investigators work crime scenes. Imagine detectives walking through a three-dimensional reconstruction of a crime scene, where every piece of evidence is tagged and mapped. They can revisit the scene multiple times, ensuring no detail is overlooked. Such technology can aid in training new investigators, offering them immersive experiences that simulate real-world scenarios without leaving the classroom. This potential for remote training and on-the-job analysis holds significant promise for jurisdictions with limited resources, democratizing the art of investigation.

One cannot discuss future trends without mentioning the role of big data and the internet of things (IoT). As devices become increasingly interconnected, they generate massive amounts of data that can be harnessed for criminal investigations. Consider smart home devices, phones, and cars, all contributing streams of information update-by-update. When pieced together, these data streams form a comprehensive tapestry of events, assisting investigators in constructing timelines and verifying alibis with precision. This vast data reservoir helps identify and track movements, providing real-time insights that might have once taken days or weeks to uncover.

Additionally, blockchain technology has the potential to revolutionize how evidence is handled. Imagine a system where every piece of evidence is logged on an immutable ledger, its chain of custody transparent and traceable. This assures that evidence presented in court hasn't been tampered with and boosts public confidence in legal outcomes. Blockchain can as well streamline inter-agency collaborations by providing secure, verifiable access to shared case files, enhancing international cooperation in investigations through secure and trusted channels.

Cybersecurity is becoming increasingly pivotal in the realm of criminal investigations, especially with the rise in cybercrime. As criminals grow more tech-savvy, investigators must stay one step ahead, armed with advanced cybersecurity protocols and tools to combat digital threats. Future trends indicate a growing emphasis on protecting critical infrastructure and private data from cyber threats, with forensic experts specializing more in digital domains. Encryption, digital rights management, and new cryptographic techniques will likely evolve to counteract sophisticated cybercrimes.

The ethics of surveillance and data gathering will continue to be a focal point of discussion. As technology facilitates more invasive means of monitoring, balancing effective criminal investigations with civil liberties is imperative. Future technologies hold tremendous potential for public safety, yet they come with a responsibility to protect individual rights. Striking this balance will shape legislative frameworks, influencing both technological deployment and the ethical parameters of investigation.

Pursuing future trends, there is also the potential to democratize access to crime-solving tools. Open-source investigative solutions could empower smaller law enforcement agencies and private investigators, leveling the playing field. By harnessing online platforms and communities, detectives can remotely collaborate, exchange techniques, and crowdsource solutions to complex cases, breaking down jurisdictional barriers and promoting a more collaborative approach to crime-solving.

One cannot overlook the human element that remains central to these future advancements. Despite technological advancements, the intuitive aspect of investigation—the human detective's insight and judgment—remains irreplaceable. Skilled investigators must adapt to these new tools, integrating them with traditional investigative techniques to craft a composite approach that embraces both innovation and experience. Training programs will need to evolve, ensuring that emerging investigators are not only tech-savvy but also possess the analytical skills to interpret and utilize technology effectively.

As we peer into the future of criminal investigation, it's clear that the role of technology is not just as a tool but as a transformative force. This evolution signifies not a replacement for human detectives but a powerful ally in the pursuit of justice. However, with this power comes responsibility. The interplay of technology and ethics will decide the path forward, guiding us to solve crimes more efficiently while respecting the fabric of society. The dance between innovation and tradition will write the next chapter in the ever-evolving story of crime-solving.

Chapter 10:
Working with Victims
and Witnesses

In the delicate dance of criminal investigation, working with victims and witnesses can be both challenging and rewarding. Their accounts often hold keys to the mysteries that detectives strive to unravel, making their cooperation crucial. Establishing trust is paramount, requiring investigators to be both empathetic listeners and strategic thinkers. It's not just about asking questions; it's about creating an environment where victims and witnesses feel safe enough to share their experiences without fear of judgment or retribution. This bond can provide insights that are not apparent at first glance, weaving together the narrative threads needed to pursue justice. Balancing sensitivity with the necessity of obtaining detailed information often involves walking a tightrope, as each case carries its own unique emotional weight and potential for trauma. Still, the rewards of cultivating these relationships extend beyond solving the case at hand, contributing to a broader understanding and resolution of the crimes that impact communities deeply.

Building Trust with Victims

Engaging with victims in the aftermath of a crime requires not just skill but a sincere understanding of human behavior and emotions. At the core of effective interaction is trust—a fragile element that, once broken, can derail the entire investigation process. Building this trust is intricate, requiring investigators to balance their need for information with the victim's vulnerabilities. But how does one start to construct such a delicate yet essential bridge?

First and foremost, the initial point of contact is crucial. Victims are often in a state of shock, overwhelmed by fear, confusion, and distress. An investigator's calm presence and empathetic demeanor can begin to ease their apprehension. Tone of voice plays a significant role; a soft-spoken, patient approach can make victims feel more comfortable and understood. Avoiding jargon or overwhelming them with technical questions right away respects their need to process what has happened.

Listening—or rather, active listening—is an investigator's most powerful tool. This isn't just about hearing words; it's about understanding the emotions and context behind those words. Victims need to feel that their stories matter and that those stories are heard without judgment. Let them set the pace, especially in the early conversations. Interruptions or insistent pressing for details can shatter the delicate threads of trust that are slowly beginning to form.

Trust is also about transparency. It's vital for victims to understand the process they are now a part of. Explaining what to expect, the timeline of events, and even potential outcomes builds confidence. This doesn't mean making promises that can't be kept, but offering a realistic yet hopeful outlook can make all the difference in how a victim perceives the justice system.

Another fundamental aspect of trust-building is confidentiality. Victims need assurance that their stories won't be exposed to people who have no business hearing them. They must feel secure that the information they provide will be used sensitively and professionally. Stressing the measures taken to protect their identities can alleviate anxieties about possible repercussions they might fear, especially in cases involving domestic violence or organized crime.

Cultural competence is often overlooked, but it's essential in building trust. Each victim comes with their background, culture, and personal history, all influencing their interaction with law enforcement. Understanding and respecting these differences can prevent misunderstandings and foster a more respectful dialogue. Investigators should be aware of their own biases and strive to approach each case with cultural sensitivity and an open mind.

Building rapport goes hand in hand with showing empathy. Validating a victim's feelings, acknowledging their trauma, and refraining from minimizing their experience is crucial. Sometimes, an investigator's role is as much about being a compassionate listener as it is about fact-finding. This emotional support can empower victims, making them more willing to engage and provide crucial information needed for the case.

While trust is constructed one step at a time, it can be dismantled with surprising ease. Any sign of complacency or dismissiveness can undo days, even weeks, of careful relationship-building. Consistency is key. Being attentive, following up on promises, and maintaining open lines of communication reinforce the connection between victim and investigator.

The human element of investigation often contrasts sharply with the procedural and fact-based aspects of policing. But it's this element that can unlock doors otherwise sealed shut. Victims who trust their investigators are more likely to cooperate, providing insights and details that might otherwise remain buried in the recesses of traumatic memory.

Ultimately, building trust with victims is not just about solving a case—it's about restoring a semblance of control and dignity to individuals whose lives have been upended. When handled with care, these relationships can render justice not solely a matter of retribution, but a process of healing and closure, benefiting both the victim and society at large.

Witness Protection Programs

The intricate dance of justice often hinges on the courage and cooperation of witnesses—ordinary people suddenly thrust into extraordinary situations. Their testimonies can make or break a case, setting a criminal free or ensuring that justice is served. But stepping forward to testify can come at a steep personal cost. Fear for their safety and repercussions from those they've bravely stood against can be a chilling deterrent. Enter the world of Witness Protection Programs, a sanctuary for those caught in the crosshairs of crime.

At their core, Witness Protection Programs are designed to safeguard the lives and identities of key witnesses. When someone decides to testify, they might not fully grasp the peril they're putting themselves in. Criminals are known to go to great lengths to protect themselves, and eliminating a witness is not beyond their means. The program acts as both shield and sword, protecting witnesses while arming them with the courage to help authorities bring criminals to justice.

Formally established in 1970 with the passing of the Organized Crime Control Act, the concept of witness protection had already been an informal practice in some law enforcement circles. The program's history is rich with stories of individuals who were whisked away under the anonymity of new aliases and relocated to different towns or even countries. Over time, these measures have been refined into a comprehensive system that aims to provide a full scope of support—not just for the witnesses but for their families as well.

The Process of Enrollment in a Witness Protection Program is as daunting as it is vital. It begins with the assessment of the witness's situation and the potential threat they face. This involves a meticulous risk analysis, taking into account the nature of the crime, the influence of the accused, and any intelligence that suggests a credible threat. If the danger outweighs the cost of losing their testimony, induction into the program is cautiously offered.

Acceptance into the program catalyzes a cascade of changes. Long before the testimony is given, the witness must sever ties with their past life. This isn't merely changing a name or residing on a different street. It's the complete remaking of an identity—a monumental task that involves acquiring a new social security number, crafting an entirely believable backstory, and even altering daily habits to fit into their new life seamlessly.

While these changes can be seen as liberating, offering a second chance at life, they're also fraught with challenges. Witnesses are uprooted from all they've known, placed in unfamiliar environments without the comfort of familiar faces. It's an arduous journey of adaptation and resilience. The emotional toll cannot be overstated, often requiring psychological counseling to help cope with the isolation and identity transformation.

Within the program's umbrella, *security is paramount.* Witnesses and their families are often relocated multiple times to avoid detection. Each new relocation is shrouded in secrecy, with as few individuals as possible knowing the whereabouts or new identity of the protected person. Law enforcement agencies invest significant time and resources to ensure that each relocation is as smooth and untraceable as possible.

Despite the comprehensive measures in place, the effectiveness of Witness Protection Programs isn't solely rooted in procedural details. A large part of its success depends on the psychological strength and adaptability of the witnesses themselves. Those who thrive do so by resolutely embracing their new identities, while accepting the permanent disconnection from their past lives. It isn't simply about new names or addresses; it's about creating new connections, finding new communities, and forging new identities.

However, the program isn't infallible. There have been instances where breaches have occurred, either through a slip from the witnesses themselves or due to the relentless pursuit of those seeking retribution. Such breaches, although rare, are stark reminders of the ever-present danger and underline the constant need for vigilance and adaptation within the program.

Witness Protection Programs have been romanticized in popular culture and true crime narratives, often depicting dramatic relocations and identity shifts. Yet, beneath this veneer lies a profound goal: upholding justice while preserving life. It's a delicate balance of judiciary necessity and human compassion.

The moral complexities surrounding these programs are myriad. On one hand, they symbolize a government's commitment to protect those who courageously aid in criminal investigations. On the other, they raise philosophical questions about identity, belonging, and the extent of governmental intervention in reshaping personal lives.

The World Beyond Witness Protection is a terrain filled with uncertainty. Many former witnesses find ways to re-establish a sense of normalcy post-program. They carry with them the knowledge that their risky decision contributed to something greater than themselves—justice. Nevertheless, some struggle to shine in their newfound lives, perpetually haunted by their invisible tether to the past.

It's essential to underscore the pivotal role Witness Protection Programs play in the larger landscape of crime-solving. These programs are lifelines for justice systems worldwide, ensuring that fear doesn't silence truth. The safety net they provide not only enables witnesses to stand up and speak out but also fortifies the judicial process by ensuring that crimes, often perpetrated in shadows, are brought to light.

In the relentless pursuit of justice, Witness Protection Programs remain an unsung hero of sorts—operating quietly in the background, offering sanctuary to those who risk it all to make what's wrong, right again. Their existence is a testament to the fact that every story has more than one hero, and sometimes, the bravest are those who are willing to leave everything behind to do what's right.

Chapter 11:
Media and Public Perception

In the tangled web of crime-solving, the media often plays an enigmatic role, shaping public perception and, at times, complicating investigations. The press can be both ally and adversary, shedding light on cold cases or driving a frenzy that muddles facts. Detectives and investigators must tread carefully, balancing transparency with the need for confidentiality, to maintain the integrity of their work without compromising leads or witnesses. Public opinion, fueled by sensational headlines and speculation, can sway the course of justice, impacting jury opinions and the pressure to secure arrests. Seasoned investigators know that adeptly managing media relations is as crucial as deciphering clues at a crime scene. Missteps can lead to amplified scrutiny or undue influence, underlining the need for a strategic approach in navigating this complex landscape where every word, image, and soundbite carries weight.

Handling Media Relations

Managing media relations in the world of criminal investigation is a delicate dance, one often fraught with both peril and opportunity. The media can serve as an ally, a crucial conduit for appealing to the public for information or cooperation, while at other times it can seem like an unforgiving mirror, magnifying perceived missteps and shaping public opinion in ways that can complicate a case.

Effective handling of media relations requires foresight, strategy, and an intricate understanding of both the journalistic landscape and the specific circumstances of the case in question. A well-thought-out media strategy can help investigators control the narrative and communicate essential information without compromising the integrity of the investigation.

At the heart of this task is the press release. Drafting a succinct and carefully worded statement is key to ensuring that the information disseminated is accurate and serves the investigation's needs. It should balance transparency with confidentiality, ensuring that only details that won't jeopardize the investigation are shared.

Investigation teams often designate a media liaison. This individual, typically someone with a background in both law enforcement and public affairs, acts as the bridge between the investigators and the media. Their role involves not just the dissemination of information, but also managing media queries, organizing press conferences, and often serving as the face of the investigation.

The timing of media releases is equally crucial. Releasing information too early can lead to a leak that compromises the investigation. Too late, and public interest—and potential witness memory—may fade. Striking this balance requires careful planning and often hinges on the progress of the investigation itself.

Handling media doesn't just involve speaking to journalists; listening to them is equally important. Reporters often gather extensive information, and while their motives may be focused on crafting a compelling story, this information can sometimes offer new leads or insights.

Media relations extend beyond traditional news outlets. In today's digital age, social media platforms have become critical avenues for sharing information. They can amplify messages quickly, reaching vast audiences. However, this comes with the challenge of misinformation spreading just as rapidly. Having a strategy in place for countering false information and managing digital communication is essential.

Public perceptions molded by media portrayals can significantly impact investigations. This is seen vividly in high-profile cases where the media frenzy becomes part of the narrative. Public opinion can sway jury pools, impact witness willingness to come forward, or even affect strategic decisions made by prosecution and defense teams.

In some scenarios, media involvement helps resolve cases. There are instances where broadcasting certain case details brings forth new witnesses or previously withheld information. A case's media exposure can sometimes be a catalyst that leads to its breakthrough.

Law enforcement must also tactfully handle the so-called " trial by media." Sometimes, intense media scrutiny can lead to premature judgments by the public. Managing such landscapes requires not only skill but also an unwavering commitment to preserving the principles of justice.

Alongside traditional challenges, the rise of citizen journalism and smartphone ubiquity adds layers of complexity. Eyewitness footage can capture crucial moments, but it can also be misinterpreted, leading to incorrect narratives gaining traction. Addressing these requires not only engaging with traditional media but also having strategies to communicate directly with the public, often utilizing social media.

In many ways, effectively managing media relations boils down to credibility and trust. Law enforcement agencies must be seen as reliable sources of information. This trust is built over time and can be easily eroded by misinformation or lack of transparency.

As true crime enthusiasts and investigators well know, the interplay between media, public perception, and criminal investigations is rich with complexity. Whether it's defusing the glare of the spotlight or strategically harnessing it to aid in solving cases, the relationship remains an essential piece of the criminal investigation puzzle.

Impact of Public Opinion on Cases

As we delve into the intricate dance between media, public perception, and criminal investigations, it becomes clear that public opinion can swing like a pendulum, affecting cases in multifaceted ways. In high-profile cases, the court of public opinion often runs parallel to the legal proceedings, sometimes interfering with the impartiality of justice. Whether through sensationalized reporting or social media campaigns, public opinion can pressure all players in the judicial system.

One of the most significant impacts of public opinion is how it shapes the narrative around a case, often from the earliest moments. Before a trial begins, many have already formed opinions based solely on media snippets or emotionally charged headlines. This biases not only those consuming the information but also affects potential jurors. Selecting an impartial jury becomes a Herculean task when the public's preconceived notions are so prevalent.

The role of media in molding public perception cannot be overstated. As 24-hour news cycles churn out story after story, the pressure to attract viewers drives outlets to prioritize sensationalism over accuracy. Misleading information can incite public outcry, prompting law enforcement and prosecuting agencies to act hastily, occasionally prioritizing a quick resolution over a thorough investigation. In some instances, this rush can lead to wrongful arrests or convictions.

Public opinion isn't a singular force; it's a complex amalgamation of personal biases, cultural contexts, and the media's narrative. Social media amplifies these dynamics immensely, giving every individual a channel to express opinions instantly. Viral posts can sway thousands, if not millions, within hours. Such rapid dissemination of opinions can exert undue pressure on legal entities to act in alignment with the public's expectations—even if those expectations are misguided or uniformed.

Consider the case of a missing person, thrust into the media spotlight. Public opinion can drive volunteer efforts and crowd-sourced investigations, bringing resources and attention that might otherwise be unavailable. Yet, when the same public veers into a vitriolic frenzy—where assumptions turn into mob behavior—the risks multiply. Innocent individuals can become targets of harassment based solely on circumstantial evidence misconstrued by amateur sleuths.

When law enforcement agencies face intense scrutiny from the public, the nature of their work changes. Officers and detectives may become more reticent or defensive, misinterpreting criticism as a lack of trust. This tension complicates the already arduous task of building community relations essential for an effective investigation. Transparency becomes a double-edged sword; while openness can foster trust, it can also leave room for misinterpretation and misjudgment.

Nonetheless, public opinion doesn't always interfere negatively. There are cases where a community's persistent demand for justice can resuscitate cold cases attracting renewed efforts from law enforcement. Public outcry can highlight systemic issues within investigative or judicial processes, prompting reforms. It's crucial to acknowledge that without public vigilance, some injustices might remain unexamined.

The intersection of public opinion and race is another area where significant friction exists. High-profile cases involving racial issues often see polarized public reactions, where opinion intersects with broader societal tensions. Such cases become arenas not just for legal battles but cultural ones, reframing the perception of justice in the public eye.

Furthermore, the impact of public opinion extends to the individuals at the heart of these cases—victims and accused alike. Before any verdict is reached in court, the people involved endure judgments rendered by the masses. Victims might face skepticism or unwarranted scrutiny, while suspects, though legally innocent until proven guilty, often find themselves convicted in the public's eye long before a trial starts.

This widespread phenomenon has prompted some judicial systems to consider reforms, such as anonymous juries or changes in gag order guidelines, aiming to insulate legal proceedings from prejudicial public opinions. The challenge lies in balancing transparency in the justice system with the need to safeguard it from the court of public opinion. Yet, these measures are not foolproof and often contend with the ongoing evolution of media and digital platforms.

Ultimately, the interplay between media, public opinion, and the justice system reflects broader societal values and tensions. It reveals the need for a more discerning public and a responsible media infrastructure. True neutrality is elusive; however, striving towards a more informed and measured public discourse remains crucial for just and fair trials.

Chapter 12:
Global Perspectives
on Crime-Solving

In an increasingly interconnected world, the realm of criminal investigation is expanding beyond borders, drawing upon diverse methodologies developed across continents. Investigators now harness international cooperation, navigating cultural complexities and legal differences to tackle complex cases. These global partnerships often lead to groundbreaking collaborations, where crime-solving techniques transcend traditional boundaries and are enriched by diverse perspectives. For instance, detectives in Europe might share their expertise on cybercrime, which complements forensic methodologies advanced in Asia, while African countries contribute invaluable insights into community-based intelligence. Case studies from around the world highlight how these cross-cultural approaches not only enhance the effectiveness of investigations but also underscore the importance of adaptability and cultural sensitivity in crime-solving. As detectives swap insights and strategies, a new, global crime-solving tapestry emerges, marked by shared knowledge and mutual respect. This chapter delves deeply into these international successes, revealing how a collective approach to justice is reshaping the future of criminal investigation.

International Cooperation in Investigations

In an increasingly interconnected world, international cooperation in criminal investigations has become not just a convenience but a necessity. The rise of transnational crimes such as human trafficking, cybercrime, and terrorism has made it clear that no nation can tackle these issues in isolation. Effective international cooperation bridges the gaps between jurisdictions, legal systems, and cultures, forming a global tapestry of law enforcement collaboration.

The complexity of international investigations demands a well-coordinated approach that respects the legal frameworks of the countries involved. At the heart of this cooperation are treaties and agreements such as Mutual Legal Assistance Treaties (MLATs), which provide a formal basis for requesting and providing assistance in gathering evidence and extraditing suspects. These treaties establish protocols that ensure requests are handled efficiently and with due regard to jurisdictional sovereignty and legal standards.

Yet, collaboration often extends beyond formal agreements. Informal networks and personal relationships between law enforcement officials play a crucial role in expediting processes that might otherwise be mired in bureaucracy. Interpol, with its 195 member countries, stands as a testament to this informal yet vital form of cooperation. Through its global policing networks and databases, Interpol facilitates the sharing of critical intelligence, helping authorities anticipate and react to criminal activities that cross borders.

Particularly illustrative of international cooperation is the European Union's Europol, which functions to enhance the effectiveness of member states in preventing and combating organized crime. Its Joint Investigation Teams (JITs) bring together law enforcement from different countries to work on cases that cross national boundaries. This collaboration allows for direct communication and cooperation, eliminating delays and increasing efficiency in tackling complex cases.

Despite the progress, challenges remain. Differences in legal systems, language barriers, and varying levels of resources can pose significant hurdles. Procedures that are second nature in one country's legal system may be entirely foreign to another, necessitating a patient, educated approach to solve these institutional labyrinths. Ensuring that all parties uphold basic human rights and legal standards remains a priority and a challenge.

Consider the multi-national effort in counter-terrorism operations, where intelligence sharing is paramount. The success of these operations often hinges on the ability to provide real-time data about potential threats. However, this level of cooperation requires building trust—both between nations and within agencies—and is not without its issues of data privacy and sovereignty.

Meanwhile, cybercrime presents its own unique set of challenges. The internet knows no borders, and cybercriminals exploit jurisdictional loopholes to evade capture. Here, international cooperation is often facilitated by specialized task forces that monitor and respond to digital threats. The Council of Europe's Convention on Cybercrime, also known as the Budapest Convention, is an essential framework that guides nations in harmonizing their cybercrime laws and fostering collaboration.

On a practical level, the challenges of language, time zone differences, and cultural variations can't be overlooked. Effective communication is paramount, requiring a careful, sensitive approach to ensure all parties feel respected and understood. Language specialists, technology that breaks down language barriers, and cultural liaisons become indispensable tools in this global effort.

Another dimension to international cooperation involves training and capacity building. Wealthier nations often provide resources and expertise to help bolster the investigative capabilities of less developed countries. This exchange of knowledge not only improves global security but fosters goodwill and mutual respect among law enforcement agencies.

Strategically, the importance of international cooperation is underscored by high-profile cases that would have been impossible to solve without such collaboration. Take, for instance, the dismantling of international drug cartels or the tracking down of notorious fugitives. These successes are often publicized, serving to reassure the public and reaffirm the value of a cohesive global approach to crime-solving.

While the benefits of international cooperation are clear, it's an evolving practice that must adapt to the ever-changing landscape of crime. As technology advances and criminals become more sophisticated, so too must the strategies and frameworks that underpin international cooperation. New treaties, cross-border initiatives, and technological innovations will shape the future of global crime-solving efforts, steering the international community towards more seamless, integrated systems of justice.

The journey of building effective international partnerships is ongoing, but the progress made thus far is encouraging. With continued dedication to overcoming the challenges of cooperation, the global community moves closer to a future where justice knows no boundaries.

Case Studies from Around the World

In the realm of crime-solving, the world offers a diverse tapestry of approaches and outcomes, all shaped by cultural, legal, and technological factors unique to each region. These cases highlight how investigative strategies can vary widely, and yet, somehow, converge towards a common goal: justice.

Starting in Europe, the notorious Whitechapel murders of the late 19th century continue to baffle experts and amateur sleuths alike.

Despite the passage of time, the identity of Jack the Ripper remains a mystery, yet the case serves as a rich study in early forensic approaches and the public's burgeoning interest in criminal investigations. It was among the first instances where crime scene photography was utilized, and it highlighted the need for a systematic approach in documenting crime scenes.

Moving southeast, the investigation into the murders of Gianni Versace in Miami and Anna Lindh in Stockholm exemplifies how developments in DNA technology transformed the way crimes are solved. Versace's case was critical in demonstrating the importance of building psychological profiles of killers, exemplified by Andrew Cunanan's depiction as a spree killer. Conversely, Lindh's case put the spotlight on surveillance technology, with footage playing a prominent role in apprehending the suspect.

The Middle East presents a contrasting backdrop with the infamous case of the Dubai assassination in 2010. This case involved a network of covert operatives whose actions were pieced together through painstaking review of surveillance footage from more than a dozen hotels and airports. The strategic router of different teams showcased not just the meticulous nature of high-stakes crime operations, but also emphasized the critical role international cooperation plays in resolving such cases.

In Asia, the handling of the 2008 Mumbai attacks offers an invaluable insight into crisis management and hostage negotiations in the face of terrorism. This complex operation required coordination across local and national police, military, and intelligence agencies, both within and outside India. The global response underscored the necessity of having an integrated framework to handle emergency situations, one that includes rapid intelligence gathering, swift communication channels, and public safety strategies.

Down under in Australia, the disappearance of Peter Falconio in the Northern Territory illuminated the challenges of investigating crimes in remote areas. The harsh and expansive Outback tested conventional crime-solving techniques, demanding innovation and robustness from the investigators working amid logistical and environmental hurdles. The integration of forensic evidence like DNA from cigarette butts found at the scene was groundbreaking at the time, ultimately leading to a conviction despite the area's desolation and lack of direct witnesses.

Across the ocean, Latin America provides another layer of investigative complexity. The murders of indigenous women along the US-Mexico border serve as a haunting reminder of systemic issues faced in crime investigations. Socioeconomic challenges and geopolitical tensions highlight the struggles faced by investigators attempting to pursue justice amidst limited resources and political constraints. Yet, these cases have sparked a broader movement for improved cross-border cooperation and legal reforms.

In Africa, the response to the Rhino horn poaching crisis in South Africa reflects the intersection of conservation and crime-solving. Here, forensic science has expanded to include environmental forensics, where DNA tracking and anti-poaching technologies are employed to trace the origins of illegal wildlife trade. These methods provide a novel glimpse into how conventional investigative procedures adapt to address non-traditional criminal activities.

Gazing northwards, Canada's infamous Highway of Tears serves as a stark illustration of how isolated geographical regions complicate crime-solving endeavors. This stretch of road has been the site of numerous unsolved disappearances, with difficult terrain and harsh weather conditions only adding to the challenge. Investigators have since implemented sophisticated data analysis techniques to identify patterns and connect victims, marking an evolution in how technology aids in resolving longstanding cases.

Finally, the case of Madeleine McCann in Portugal's Algarve region continues to capture global attention. Her disappearance in 2007 showcases the complications that arise in international investigations, especially concerning jurisdictional differences. This case underscores the absolute necessity for coordination and communication across borders to streamline investigative efforts and manage the interplay between media influence, public sentiment, and procedural integrity.

These cases, taken from the world over, offer invaluable lessons in crime-solving. They emphasize the necessity of adapting investigative strategies to the unique challenges posed by each cultural and geographical context. As global partnerships continue to evolve, the quest for solving crimes remains an intricate blend of science, intuition, and cooperation, reshaping the landscape of criminal investigations one lesson at a time.

Conclusion

Wrapping up a journey that dives deep into the realms of crime-solving, we find ourselves illuminated by the intricate dance of intellect, science, and human experience. Those absorbed in the world of criminal investigations understand that at its core, it's a relentless quest for truth. This book has traversed numerous facets—from the evolution of investigative techniques to the profound impact of technology—each playing a pivotal role in transforming mere incidents into stories of justice.

The threads that bind every chapter are sewn with the understanding that every step, every decision, and every breakthrough hinges on the foundational knowledge of criminal investigation. The fundamentals aren't just stepping stones; they're the bedrock upon which entire careers are built. As you've learned, the merging of traditional methods with modern, cutting-edge technology doesn't just enhance investigations; it redefines them. With forensic science becoming ever more sophisticated, its pivotal role is undisputed. It moves the dial from speculation to certainty, often standing as the turning point in what seemed to be unsolvable enigmas.

The real-world implications of these advancements cannot be overstated. With each case study, we've seen how lives are impacted and justice served through perseverance and innovation. The path from hypothesis at a crime scene to gathering the last piece of damning evidence is rarely straight or simple. It involves a symphony of strategies, each note contributing to the melody of revelation.

Documenting crime scenes, collecting evidence, and employing effective interview strategies form this nuanced symphony.

Our deep dive into interrogation techniques reveals the psychological ballet that dances around human perception and truth. Understanding human nature's complexities makes or breaks the effectiveness of these encounters. The narrative is far from linear, demanding empathy, insight, and a rigorous understanding of the human psyche to unravel the truth.

Equally compelling is the exploration of the edges of legality and ethics. The law serves as both map and boundary for investigators navigating complex terrains. These legal frameworks don't merely constrain; they empower by providing a ethical guideline, ensuring that justice, when served, is indisputable. As investigators face burgeoning tech challenges, they're forced to grapple with ever-growing mountains of digital data. Digital forensics, while a boon, demands precision and accuracy to transform zeros and ones into narratives that speak truth.

Yet, not all trails lead to quick resolution. Cold cases remind us of justice's endurance. They teach patience and the value of persistent interrogation, compelling us to revisit the past with fresh eyes and new tools. As we reconsider these unsolved mysteries, the past and present converge, offering a renewed chance for resolution.

There's a human side too. Engaging with victims and witnesses, extending empathy and protection, building relationships rooted in trust—these elements are as critical as any scientific breakthrough. And when the media lens magnifies pressure, handling public perception becomes a delicate art. The narrative of crime and justice doesn't just exist in hushed courtrooms or quietly in lab results; it finds its voice in public opinion and media portrayals.

Globally, crime-solving approaches vary, yet the ultimate objective remains unchanged: achieving justice. International case studies highlight that while methodologies might differ, the pursuit of truth transcends borders. As the landscape of criminal investigation evolves, so must those who partake in its pursuit. While the future of technology beckons with promises of even greater precision, it's the human element that will continue to guide these advances.

The tapestry of criminal investigation is woven with many threads—each chapter in this book contributing to a richer understanding of this world. As enthusiasts, detectives, and everyday citizens, there is much to learn and apply. As we conclude, we are reminded that each solution often prompts new questions, and it's in that cycle of curiosity and resolution that the true art and science of investigation come to life.

Glossary of Terms

Understanding the language of criminal investigation is crucial. Here's a glossary that will serve as your companion, breaking down essential terms into digestible explanations. This section aims to demystify the often complex terminology found in the world of crime-solving.

Accomplice

Someone who actively participates in the commission of a crime, assisting the main perpetrator before, during, or after the criminal act.

Alibi

An assertion by an accused person that they were elsewhere when a crime was committed, supported by evidence such as witness statements or other verification.

Chain of Custody

A documented process that tracks the collection, handling, and storage of evidence from the crime scene to the courtroom, ensuring integrity and reliability.

Circumstantial Evidence

Evidence that relies on an inference to connect it to a conclusion of fact, such as a fingerprint at the scene of a crime. While not direct proof, it can be compelling in supporting a case.

DNA Profiling

A forensic technique used to identify individuals by analyzing the unique genetic makeup found in their biological samples. Critical in solving cases with limited physical evidence.

Felony

A serious crime typically punishable by imprisonment for more than one year or by death. Examples include murder, rape, and kidnapping.

Interrogation

The formal questioning of a suspect, witness, or victim, usually conducted by law enforcement to gather facts or obtain a confession.

Modus Operandi (M.O.)

The characteristic method or pattern of behavior that a criminal uses during the commission of a crime, offering insights into their skills and psychological profile.

Probable Cause

A reasonable basis for believing that a crime may have been committed, a necessary threshold that law enforcement must meet to obtain warrants or make arrests.

Surveillance

The close observation of an individual or group, typically performed by law enforcement, to gather evidence of criminal activity without direct interaction.

Witness Protection Program

A program designed to protect witnesses who are at risk due to their testimony. This can include relocation, new identities, or other security measures.

Each of these terms is a building block that supports the framework of criminal investigation. They represent the tools and concepts essential to navigating this complex but fascinating field.

Appendix:
Resources for Aspiring Detectives

Stepping into the world of criminal investigation is no small feat, and having the right resources can make a tremendous difference. Whether you're a true crime aficionado or an aspiring detective, building a toolkit of knowledge is essential. This section provides a curated list of resources that can help guide and inspire your journey into the intricacies of crime-solving.

Books and Publications

- **" Criminal Investigation: A Method for Reconstructing the Past" by James W. Osterburg and Richard H. Ward** - This comprehensive guide offers a deep dive into the methodologies and practices used by seasoned investigators.

- **" Forensic Science: From the Crime Scene to the Crime Lab" by Richard Saferstein** - A foundational text for understanding the crucial role of forensic science in modern investigations.

- " Profilers: Leading Investigators Take You Inside the Criminal Mind" by John H. Campbell and Don DeNevi - **A fascinating look into the minds of those who specialize in criminal profiling.**

- " Cold Case Research: Resources for Unidentified, Missing, and Cold Homicide Cases" by Silvia Pettem - **A must-read** for those intrigued by the challenges of cold case investigations.

Online Courses and Workshops

- **Coursera - Forensic Science: The Basics** - An online course that introduces the scientific techniques used in solving crimes.

- **edX - Introduction to International Criminal Law** - Provides insights into the legal frameworks that govern international investigations.

- **Open University - The Science of Crime Scenes** - A free course focusing on the methods used to document and analyze crime scenes.

Professional Organizations

- **International Association of Crime Analysts (IACA)** - A resource hub for crime analysts that offers training and certification programs.

- **American Academy of Forensic Sciences (AAFS)** - Provides information on the latest advancements and best practices in the field of forensic science.

Podcasts and Documentaries

- **" Criminal" Podcast** - Delving into a wide range of crime stories, this podcast offers insights into both historical and contemporary cases.

- **" Mindhunter" Documentary** - Explores the origins and development of criminal profiling at the FBI.

Networking and Conferences

- **Annual Meeting of the International Criminal Police Organization (Interpol)** - An opportunity to engage with professionals from around the world and stay updated on international crime-solving collaboration.

- **Forensic Science Symposiums** - Various symposiums held across the globe bring forensic experts together to discuss innovations and challenges in the field.

As you immerse yourself in these resources, remember that the field of criminal investigation is ever-evolving. Stay curious, remain informed, and continue honing your skills to uncover the truth behind the mysteries you seek to solve.